IVY LEAGUE FOOTBALL

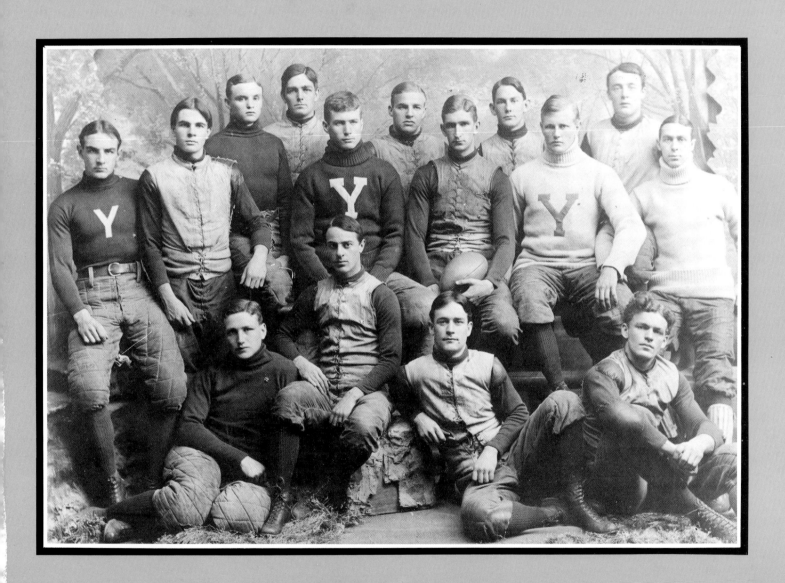

IVY LEAGUE FOOTBALL

GENERAL EDITOR: JOHN S. BOWMAN

CRESCENT

The 1988 edition published by Crescent Books, distributed by Crown Publishers, Inc.
225 Park Avenue South
New York, NY 10003

Produced by
Bison Books Corp.
15 Sherwood Avenue
Greenwich, CT 06830
USA

THOMAS G AYLESWORTH is an experienced author and editor, with over 40 books to his credit including *The World Series.*

JOSEPH BERTAGNA played ice hockey at Harvard (and coaches the Boston Bruins' goalies) and is now Executive Director of the Varsity Club at Harvard.

JANET BOND is a freelance writer who has contributed to several volumes on American history; she has family ties to both Cornell and Dartmouth.

Printed in Hong Kong

ISBN 0-517-65847-X

h g f e d c b a

MARK CURRAN was Director of Sports Information at Yale University from 1981 to 1987; a member of the Football Writers of America, he is now a freelance writer.

JIM DEGNIM is a sports writer for the *Daily Hampshire Gazette* in Northampton, Massachusetts, and covers football as well as many other sports.

BENTON MINKS, a high school English teacher by vocation, is an avid sports fan; he recently published his first book, *100 Greatest Hitters.*

Page 1: *The Yale football team of 1900.*

Previous pages: *The Tigers of Princeton versus the Quakers of the University of Pennsylvania.*

These pages: *A football game at Dartmouth in 1893.*

CONTENTS

Introduction 6

Brown University by Jim Degnim 14

Columbia University by Benton Minks 38

Cornell University by Janet Bond 56

Dartmouth College by Janet Bond 78

Harvard University by Joseph Bertagna 98

University of Pennsylvania
by Thomas G Aylesworth 130

Princeton University by Thomas G
Aylesworth 150

Yale University by Mark Curran 168

Ivy League Records 189

Index and Acknowledgments 190

INTRODUCTION

Below: 'We are ever true to Brown! For we love our college dear! And wherever we may go! We are ready with a cheer! . . .'.

Bottom right: 'Glory to Dartmouth! Loyal we sing! Now all together! MAKE THE ECHOES RING FOR DARTMOUTH!. . .'

Ivy League football: if ever three innocent words aroused passion among football fans, it is these. For many people, 'Ivy League football' evokes images that seem to have little direct bearing on events on the gridiron. There is all the ritual preceding the game, for instance – 'tailgating' in the parking lots, with gourmet meals that transcend the idea of a picnic. Or there is the choice of clothes to wear to the game – raccoon coats may no longer be quite in fashion, but stylish if casual clothing is certainly preferred.

Once inside the stadium, Ivy League football fans – mostly current students and devoted alumni – settle down with their blankets and pennants and perhaps the elegant thermos kits that have replaced the old hip flask. For the weather is definitely a part of Ivy League football – crisp autumn afternoons that usually give way well before the season ends to raw cold, even to blizzards. During the game, music and cheers resound, and if the bands and cheerleaders aren't as well-drilled as those at other college games, Ivy Leaguers make up for this in sheer spontaneity.

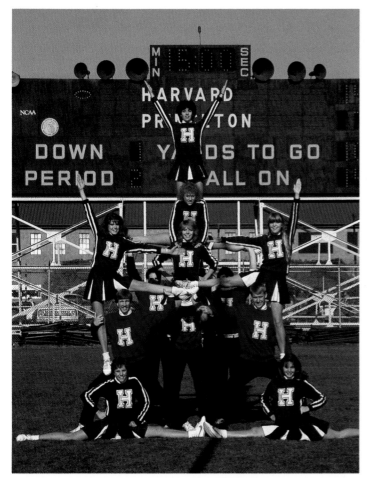

Top left: *Harvard cheerleaders in formation before the scoreboard at Harvard Stadium.*

Top right: *'Every tune, every harp and every voice/ Did every care withdraw/ Let all with one accord rejoice/ In praise of Old Nassau. . . .'*

Left: *Boaters and brass: the band of the Orange and Black belt out a tune.*

Above left: *Airborne antics by the Princeton cheering squad at Palmer Stadium.*

Above: *'Bulldog! Bulldog! Bow, wow, wow/ Eli Yale/ Bulldog! Bulldog! Bow, wow, wow/ Our team can never fail. . . .'*

Above: *The great Walter Camp, when he was Yale's team captain in 1878.*

Below: *A Winslow Homer drawing depicting a frosh-soph soccer-style match at Harvard in 1857.*

Opposite top left: *Early fisticuffs between the men of Princeton and Yale.*

Opposite top right: *The 1903 Dartmouth team poses on the snow-blanketed Green.*

Opposite bottom: *Coach Percy Haughton talks to his assistant coaches at Columbia in 1923.*

But, it might be objected, the Ivy League no longer holds a monopoly on such carryings-on. For just as the image of 'ivy-covered halls' has been extended to symbolize colleges in general, many of the ingredients of Ivy League football games have pretty much been taken up by most colleges. And yet there still seems to be something special about, if not unique to, Ivy League football games. Perhaps the closest one can come to defining it is an aura of nostalgia that hovers over such contests – the ghosts of great teams and players of years gone by, the traditions maintained by the colleges, the rivalries that go back well over a century.

The eight Ivy League schools are Brown, Columbia, Cornell, Dartmouth, Harvard, University of Pennsylvania, Princeton and Yale. They have had a long history of competing in various sports, including football, but the term 'Ivy League' was actually first applied to them in 1937 by Caswell Adams, a sportswriter on *The New York Herald Tribune*. In 1945, an 'Ivy Group Agreement' was published, setting forth several conditions (academic standards, financial aid, etc) for their football programs but not requiring them to play each other. In 1952, the eight colleges tightened up the terms of this agreement: specifically, no spring practice, no postseason or bowl games, no football clinics (for secondary schools), no scholarships just for football ability, no subsidized players. Even then, the colleges only agreed to play each other once every five years – and the University of Pennsylvania in particular pretty much went its own way.

The big change came in February 1954, when the agreement was further revised and extended to cover all sports. But football remained the heart of the Ivy League agreement, and the major new condition was that, starting in 1956, each of the colleges would have to play football against the other seven *every* season. By 1973, the sports programs and schedules involving the eight schools were so involved that they set up a full-time office and staff, formally known as the Council of Ivy Group Presidents and located in Princeton, New Jersey. Some people say that the Ivy League is not a 'true' league, but don't tell that to the staff that oversees one of the busiest programs (33 sports) and tightest agreements in intercollegiate athletics.

One irony that does strike those who have occasion to think about the history of Ivy League football is that these colleges that now seem to 'downplay' football are the very ones that first boosted football. Indeed, with the notable exception of Rutgers, the colleges involved in the early stage of the development and spread of American-style football tended to be the ones that became the Ivy League.

Of course the football being played during those early years was far removed from what Americans today know as football. Like the game that had been played in America probably since the earliest days, college football was much more like what Americans know as soccer; it then passed through a stage where it was more like what is known as rugby football. But it was primarily the colleges that would become the Ivy League that took the lead in developing American-style football. These are the crucial dates and stages in this development:

Above: *Cornell coach Maxie Baughan.*

1869 The first intercollegiate football game is played on 6 November at New Brunswick, New Jersey, by Rutgers and Princeton. Each team played 25 men at a time; the ball was a round rubber one; it was kicked or butted with the head but no throwing or running with the ball was allowed; the field was 360 by 225 feet. Rutgers won, 6 (goals) to 4. (The same teams met at Princeton a week later, when Princeton won, 8-0.)

1870 Columbia, Cornell and Yale begin to play football on their own campuses, and Columbia plays Rutgers.

1871 Harvard College students are playing a form of football known as 'the Boston game,' a bit more like rugby in that players could run short distances with the ball. Princeton forms its football club.

1872 Yale plays Columbia. Princeton plays Rutgers again, the first game under revised rules that begins to move the sport a bit more toward rugby.

1873 Yale, Columbia, Princeton and Rutgers send delegates to a meeting at the Fifth Avenue Hotel in New York City; on 19 October, as the first Intercollegiate Football Association, they draw up some new rules for what remains a soccer-like game. In particular, they agree to limit teams to 20 players – one reason that Harvard declines to participate in this association. Yale plays Princeton and Rutgers this year. Yale also plays an English team called the Eton Players;

Left: *Dartmouth fans applaud as the Green Machine hits the field.*

Above: *The Brown Bear boogies on the field at halftime.*

Opposite top: *'Give my regards to Davy/ Remember me to Teefy Crane/ Tell all the Pikers on the Hill/ That I'll be back again. . . .'*

Opposite bottom: *Eli DE Jeff Cramtton (81) prevents Harvard's Brian Bergstrom (27) from making a reception in the 1984 edition of The Game.*

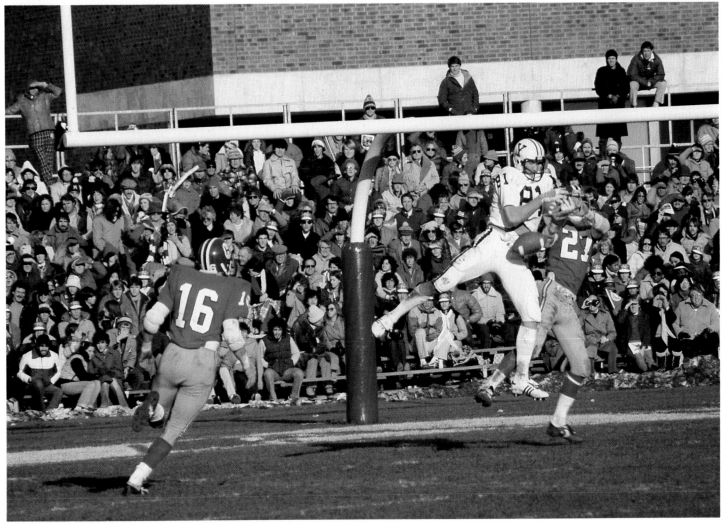

although only 11 men play for each team, the game was probably still more like modern soccer or rugby.

1874 Harvard plays the first international football games (14 and 15 May) against McGill University of Montreal; the first two games are in Cambridge, but a third is played in Montreal in the fall. The ball used was ovoid but the game was more like rugby football than modern football.

1875 Representatives of football teams at Harvard and Yale meet at Springfield, Massachusetts, on 16 October and adopt rules for a game that combines elements of soccer and rugby. On 13 November, Harvard and Yale play their first football game. (Harvard won, 4-0.)

1876 On 18 November, Harvard and Yale play their first football game using an oval ball and only 11 men per team. On 23 November, at the Massasoit House in Springfield, Massachusetts, Columbia, Harvard, Princeton, Rutgers and Yale meet to form a new Intercollegiate Football Association; they adopt rules that will bring the game closer to rugby but still allow teams to field 15 men (causing Yale to refuse to join the association). After this meeting, Princeton plays the University of Pennsylvania (the latter's first intercollegiate game) but under the old (1873) rules. (Princeton wins, 6-0.) Then Princeton plays Yale (with Yale winning, 2-0) in what is regarded as the first intercollegiate game under the new (1876) rules.

1878 Brown plays its first intercollegiate game, against Amherst College.

1880 Yale gets most of the active colleges to accept the 11-man team, and the field is reduced to 110 by 53 yards. Walter Camp, a recent Yale graduate and active in the Intercollegiate Football Association, persuades the teams to replace the rugby 'scrummage' with a more organized 'scrimmage' line; also, the ball is to be kicked back to the quarterback; and equally radical, the team in possession of the ball retains it until it is fumbled.

Below: The scene at the Yale Bowl has changed little since this photo was taken in the 1930s.

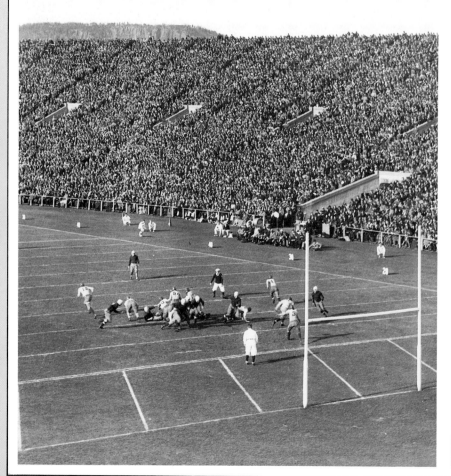

1881 Dartmouth plays its first intercollegiate game (against Amherst). The University of Michigan sends its team east to play Yale, Harvard and Princeton – the first intersectional games; Michigan introduces called signals before each play.

1882 College teams adopt the system of 'downs': on three downs, a team must move the ball at least five yards or lose 10 yards, or surrender the ball; this creates the need to draw white lines across the field, thus giving rise to the word 'gridiron.' Yale, meanwhile, has begun to concentrate on a running game.

So it was that modern American football was on its way to becoming the popular sport we know today, from grade-school leagues to the NFL. The Ivy League colleges continued to get more than their share of the spotlight during the early decades of the twentieth century, but they did serve to shape the sport, whether by sending their graduates out to coach other colleges or by building great stadiums. Gradually, though, the Ivy League colleges, through a series of decisions and priorities, came to give less emphasis to football, as other colleges committed increasing amounts of their resources to the game.

But in no way did this mean any lessening of the spirit and loyalties that have characterized the link between the Ivy League and football. True, there have always been some Ivy Leaguers who cultivate a studied indifference to the game (although it is questionable whether they make up any larger percentage than at other colleges). But once an Ivy League team takes the field, the spirit is not much different from that at all hotly-contested athletic events. The same hard work and sacrifice have gone into the practice sessions – if anything, even more, since Ivy League players must maintain their grades. There is the same desire to win, the same dedication to playing hard until the final whistle sounds. So, too, for the spectators, these Ivy League games are no less intense and festive than those played by the superpowers of college football – as intense and festive as the game introduced by Ivy League colleges over a century ago.

Below: *Halfback Phil Avila scores for the Quakers of Penn against Lehigh in 1978.*

Bottom left: *Tailback Derrick Harmon (31) moves the ball for Cornell.*

BROWN
UNIVERSITY

Founded: 1764
Location: Providence, Rhode Island
Undergraduate Enrollment: 5518
Colors: Seal Brown, Cardinal Red and White
Nickname: Bruins

Previous pages: *QB Joe Potter (17) rolls out in 1983 action against Harvard.*

Above: *The first Bruin mascot was this bear cub, who made his debut at Andrews Field in 1905.*

Rose Bowls, Heisman Trophies, and All-Americans may not be immediately associated with Brown University football by non-alumni, but all are indeed part of a tradition that began on 13 November 1878, in Amherst, Massachusetts. It was on that fall day that the Brown Football Association (wearing uniforms not yet paid for) took on the Amherst Football Association. The Amherst side won handily, but that did not discourage the Brown students from proceeding to develop the early traditions of the 'Bruins,' as their team is known.

More than 100 years later, there is a vast storehouse of memories – of Brown's trip to the Rose Bowl, of the undefeated 'Iron Men' of 1926, of the running and passing of Bill Sprackling, of Edward North Robinson (to some, the father of Brown football), of record-setting running back Bob Margarita, of the Ivy League championship team of 1976.

Then there is the pride Brown followers have felt in seeing their own become nationally famous after leaving Brown, men like one-time Brown student John Heisman, the namesake of the award given annually to the best college

football player in the country. Or Joe Paterno, the former Bruin captain who led Penn State to the 1986 national championship and is considered by many to be one of the best coaches in the country. Or Charles 'Rip' Engle, who coached Paterno at Brown before going on to Penn State and a career that earned him a place in the National Football Hall of Fame. Or W Wallace 'Wally' Wade, who first made his name as a Brown player (he was right guard on the Rose Bowl team) and went on to coach at Alabama and Duke, taking both these schools to the Rose Bowl on several occasions.

Brown's first official game was played in 1878, but it was not until 1890 that the team played a full schedule. Heisman was a student at Brown from 1887 to 1889, but there is no record of his playing football, probably because Brown did not field a team in 1887 or 1888. Heisman went on to graduate from the University of Pennsylvania, from which he also took a law degree before embarking on a coaching career that included stints at eight colleges. Needless to say, Heisman is a member of the National Football Hall of Fame.

For the record, Brown's first win came in 1886, a 70-0 victory against Providence High School. But it took football a while to catch on, owing to the college's reputation as a baseball power. (Brown won the national championship in collegiate baseball in 1896.) Football began building on this foundation at Brown thanks to an enthusiastic student named John H Lindsay, who served as captain and coach in 1890 when Brown played its first full schedule and wound up with two wins, four losses, and one tie. Lindsay was the captain and coach again in 1891 as Brown went 4-6-0.

Meanwhile, the president of the college, Benjamin Andrews, was becoming interested in this relatively novel sport, and this greatly helped the cause. In 1892 Brown hired its first full-time coach, and the team was given its first on-campus home, at Lincoln Field.

That year also marked the beginning of the Edward North 'Robbie' Robinson era at Brown. A freshman fullback in 1892, Robinson scored the lone touchdown to give Brown its first big win, a 6-0 decision against Wesleyan. Robinson would go on to coach more seasons (24) and win more games at Brown than any other man before retiring after the 1925 season. The 1896 season was also noteworthy because of the senior who served as team manager: John D Rockefeller, Jr.

In 1904, Theodore Francis Green, a Brown alumnus, was the first to suggest the school use a bear as its mascot. The Bruin made its first appearance in 1905, prowling the sidelines

during a 24-6 loss to Dartmouth. Actual bear cubs appeared as mascots during Brown games for many years before being replaced by a costume bear in 1963.

By 1905 Brown had moved to Andrews Field (named for the former president), which would be its home through the 1924 season. And it was during the early years of this century that Brown football began picking up steam. In 1906 back John Mayhew became the first Bruin to be named to Walter Camp's All-America first team. Right on the heels of Mayhew came perhaps the greatest player in Brown history, brash quarterback Bill Sprackling.

Equally gifted as a passer, runner and kicker, the 150-pound Sprackling remains the only three-time All-American in Brown annals (1909, 1910 and 1911). Sprackling, who often played without a helmet or shoulder pads, was one of the pioneers of the forward pass. During his starry career he threw 11 touchdown passes, an unusually high number for that era. Sprackling's greatest single game came in a 21-0 win against Yale in 1910, Brown's first victory over the Elis (or 'Blues,' as Yale was also called in those days) in 30 years and 17

Top: *The first Brown football team, which was formed in 1878.*

Above: *John Hathaway Lindsay, the player/coach who led the Brown team through their first full schedule in 1890.*

Left: *John W Heisman played football on club teams at Brown from 1887 to 1889. One of football's great innovators, he coached at Penn from 1920 to 1922.*

Above: *Elisha Benjamin Andrews, Brown's president from 1889 to 1898, helped to establish football as a varsity sport.*

Right: *Edward North Robinson was a fullback at Brown from 1892 to 1896 and returned to coach in 1898. In 24 seasons (1898-1901, 1904-07, 1910-25) he compiled a 140-82-12 record, the winningest in Brown history. He was elected to the National Football Hall of Fame in 1955.*

games. Sprackling, a member of the National Football Hall of Fame, accounted for 456 all-purpose yards in the game.

Brown splashed onto the national scene in 1915 with its Rose Bowl invitation, despite an unremarkable 5-3-1 record. The Bruins did own a 3-0 win over Yale, which at the time gave a team credibility, especially in the West. The win over Yale had a strange twist to it: the winning points came on a 25-yard field goal by captain Harold 'Buzz' Andrews, the only field goal he attempted during his Brown career.

Led by its dazzling running back, Frederick 'Fritz' Pollard, Brown made the five-day train trip to California to meet Washington State on 1 January 1916. A 5-foot 8-inch, 150-pound halfback, Pollard was black – a rarity in college football in those days. He came to Providence from Chicago and worked his way through school pressing clothes. On the field, his shifty running often left opponents out to dry. Pollard was one of the first blacks named to Walter Camp's All-America first team when he earned that distinction in 1916.

Upon arriving at Pasadena's Hotel Raymond, the Bruins were greeted by the owner, Walter Raymond – a Harvard man – dressed in a complete Crimson football outfit, helmet included. The welcome was not quite as cordial for Pollard, who was told by a desk clerk that other arrangements would be made for his lodging. Only when the Brown team threatened to leave was the star runner given a room. Pollard also had his troubles with a muddy field on game day in the Rose Bowl, as Washington State's Cougars claimed a 14-0 victory.

Even though the game ran up an $11,000 deficit, Brown received its guarantee of $5,000 and upon returning to Providence's Union Station seven days later, the Brown contingent told a reporter from the *Providence Journal* that it had been a 'corking' trip. Brown had a part in history by playing in that Rose Bowl because, despite its financial problems, organizers decided that a football game would be part of the 'Tournament of Roses' festival every year. Prior to 1916, there had been one football game held as part of the festivities, but Michigan so badly outclassed Stanford in that 1902 matchup that officials abandoned the idea of football for several years, turning instead to other attractions, among them chariot racing.

In addition to Pollard, Wade and Andrews, the other starters on the Rose Bowl team were Josh Weeks, Mark Farnum, Ken Sprague, Edgar 'Spike' Staff, Ray Ward, John Butler, Clair Purdy and Harold Saxton. The next sea-

Above: *The 1896 team was managed by John D Rockefeller, Jr (wearing black hat).*

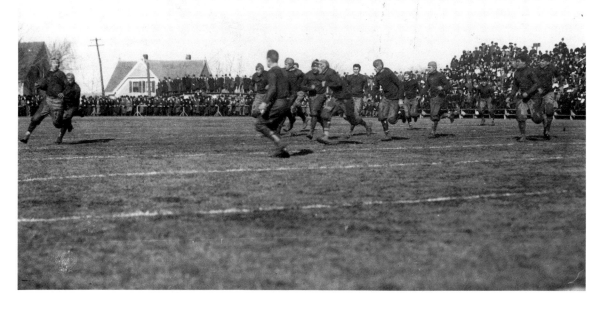

Above: *Game action on Andrews Field, 1911.*

son Pollard led one of Brown's best teams ever to wins over Harvard and Yale en route to an 8-1 season. Brown remained very successful for the next nine years, enjoying eight winning seasons.

One of the top players of the mid-1920s was Adolph 'Dolph' Eckstein, whom many call the Bruins' top all-time center. Eckstein managed to maintain a high level of performance despite his unusual habit of giving blood in exchange for money on the day of a game or the day before, a practice which doubtless irked Coach Robinson.

In 1925 the team dedicated the new

Above: The program from the 1916 Tournament of Roses game. The Bruins were the first Eastern school to be invited to Pasadena, on the strength of a 5-3-1 season in which they outscored their opponents 167-32. They were held scoreless there by the Washington State Cougars, 14-0.

Right: Quarterback Bill Sprackling was the star of the Brown team from 1909-11. A speedy runner, accurate passer and effective dropkicker, he led Brown to a 15-6 victory over the Carlisle Indians and Jim Thorpe and a spectacular 21-0 win over Yale in 1910. Masterly under pressure and an inspiring leader, 'Sprack' remains Brown's only three-time All-American.

Above: Back John Mayhew was the first Bruin to make Walter Camp's All-America first team, in 1906.

Opposite top: The 1915 Brown eleven (l-r, line) Josh Weeks, Mark Farnum, Wallace Wade, Ken Sprague, Edgar J Spike, Ray Ward, John Butler; (l-r, backfield) QB Clair Purdy, Buff Andrews, Harold Saxton, Fritz Pollard.

Opposite bottom: Adolph 'Dolph' Eckstein is still regarded as one of Brown's best centers ever. He played for the Bruins in the mid-1920s.

20,000-seat Brown Stadium, designed by architect Gavin Hadden, with an all-home schedule. That season also marked the end of Robinson's legendary career, as the Bruins went 5-4-1. DeOrmond 'Tuss' McLaughry, from Amherst, succeeded Robinson in 1926 and fielded the famous unbeaten 'Iron Men,' to this day the only Brown squad to go through the entire season without a loss. The 'Iron Men' were so named because in back-to-back wins against Yale and Dartmouth, the 11 starters played the entire 60 minutes. McLaughry said the creation of the Iron Men was quite unintentional: In the first four games of the season, he had used all 26 of his players.

On 23 October, in a 7-0 victory against Yale, the Iron Men were born. Brown's only touchdown came on a run by fullback Al Cornsweet. Dave Mishel kicked the extra point. McLaughry decided to leave the starters – Cornsweet, Mishel, captain Hal Broda, Ed Kevorkian, Lou Farber, Orland Smith, Paul Hodge, Charlie Considine, Roy Randall, Ed Lawrence and Thurston Towle – in the game

to protect the lead. A week later in Hanover, New Hampshire, the Iron Men went all the way in a 10-0 win over Dartmouth. The durable unit played all but three minutes the next week in a 21-0 win against Harvard. By this time, the Iron Men had thoroughly captured the country's imagination.

Brown entered the Thanksgiving morning season finale at home against Colgate with hopes of completing an already memorable season with a 10-0 record. When Mishel lined up for a 15-yard field goal attempt late in the fourth quarter with the score tied, 10-10, it appeared the sellout crowd of 26,000 would get its wish. But Mishel, who had made 22 of 22 extra points from just about the same spot that season, saw his kick deflect off the left upright and Brown had to settle for a tie and a 9-0-1 record, still the school's best.

Six years later, in 1932, McLaughry had a team that may have been just as good – and again Colgate played the spoiler. Led by captain Bill Gilbane, the Bruins defeated unbeaten teams in the first seven games of the season. These were heady times for Brown. Fullback Frank Gammino, who received a $100 bill from his father every time he scored a touchdown, often shared his largesse by treating his teammates to sumptuous meals at his family's Warren Hotel.

By the time Brown moved its record to 7-0 there was talk of another trip to the Rose Bowl. When a very formidable Colgate team visited Brown Stadium on Thanksgiving Day, the 32,000 fans learned why Colgate coach Andy Kerr's powerhouse had outscored the opposition, 243-0, in its previous eight victories. Colgate scored a convincing 21-0 triumph, which meant the Rose Bowl representative who sat in the stands with an invitation for the Bruins (should they win) could not offer it. Instead, Pittsburgh went West for the game, leaving Colgate and Kerr understandably upset.

Above: *The 1926 Iron Men: (l-r, line) Thurston Towle, Paul Hodge, Orland Smith, Charlie Considine, Louis Farber, Ed Kevorkian, Captain Hal Broda; (l-r, backfield) Al Cornsweet, Dave Mishel, Eddie Lawrence, Roy Randall.*

Left: *Halfback Dave Mishel, one of the 11 starters on the 1926 squad whose endurance and talent earned them the name the Iron Men.*

Opposite bottom left: *DeOrmond 'Tuss' McLaughry coached the Bruins from 1926 to 1940, and fielded the famous unbeaten Iron Men team of 1926.*

Opposite bottom right: *Fullback Frank Gammino contributed his talents to the 1932 team that compiled an 8-1 record for the season.*

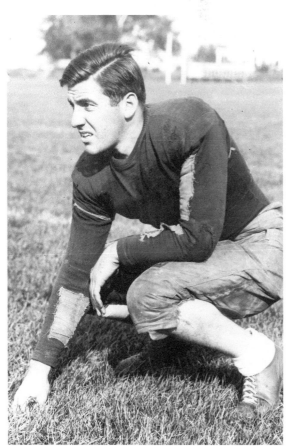

Brown's fortunes dipped for the next few seasons. In 1937, though, junior running back Irving 'Shine' Hall helped Brown post a 5-4-1 mark, including a stunning 7-6 upset of Columbia. Tom Nash caught a touchdown pass from Larry Atwell to tie the score and Hall kicked the winning point-after to beat the Lions. A year later, Hall almost singlehandedly beat Columbia and Sid Luckman, scoring 27 points in a 36-27 win. Another key performer during that period was John McLaughry, the coach's son and a top back and linebacker who went on the coach Brown from 1959 to 1966. John McLaughry also played quarterback for

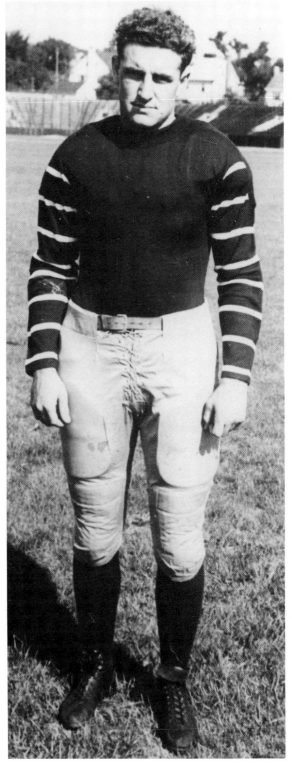

Opposite: *Joe Paterno set several records at Brown in 1949.*

Left: *Running back Irving 'Shine' Hall in 1937.*

Above: *Charles A 'Rip' Engle was head coach from 1944 to 1950.*

Top: *Star running back Bob Margarita in 1940.*

Right: *Linebacker John McLaughry in 1939.*

one season with the New York Giants.

Brown was no worse than a .500 team from 1939 to 1943. The best-known player during this stretch was a 5-foot 10-inch, 174-pound running back named Bob Margarita. Against Columbia in 1942, he rambled for 233 yards to establish a Brown single-game rushing record. In the same season against Lafayette, Margarita had a 176-yard effort, which more than 40 years later still ranked among the 10 best games by a Brown runner.

Rip Engle's first season as coach was 1944, and it took him a while to find the personnel to run his Wing-T offense. Engle endured three losing campaigns and a 4-4-1 season before closing his Brown career with a combined record of 17-3 in 1948 and 1949. The running and passing of Joe Paterno was primarily responsible for a 41-26 comeback win against Colgate on Thanksgiving Day in 1949, Engle's final game at Brown and one he called one of his four greatest victories with the Bruins. Paterno set Brown records for career interceptions with 14, return yardage on interceptions with 290 yards and career punt return yardage with 350 yards. One of Paterno's teammates, tackle Don Colo, went on to play eight years of professional football, most of it with the Cleveland Browns. No Brown alumnus has logged more time in the pros.

Alva Kelley took over as coach in 1951, and the Bruins struggled in his first three seasons. But in 1954, with honorable mention All-Americans Pete Kohut at quarterback and Harry Josephson at end, Brown posted a fine 6-2-1 record. Kelley had better-than average teams in 1956 and 1957 and capped his career at Brown with a 6-3 record in his final season in 1958, which included wins over Harvard and Yale. Paul Choquette, a two-time honorable mention All-American and a two-time All-Ivy pick, ran for 113 yards in the 35-29 decision against Yale. The quarterback on that team was Frank Finney, who led the Ivy League in passing, total offense and scoring in 1958. Bill Traub of Brown was the leading receiver in the Ivy League that year, and set a new school record with seven receptions in a single game, against Harvard.

The John McLaughry years (1959-66) were lean ones, with only one winning season. That came in 1964, when the Bruins beat Columbia on the last day of the season, 7-0, to finish at 5-4. Brown was not without outstanding individual talent during this time. John Parry, who went on to become the athletic director at Brown, was an honorable mention All-America receiver in 1963 and 1964 and set a Brown mark with 96 career catches.

During the mid-1960s, the men in seal brown and cardinal red limped through several losing seasons. A school-record 12-game losing streak was established in 1966 and 1967. One of the bright lights of the era was someone who got plenty of work: punter Joe Randall. Twice an All-Ivy selection, Randall set Brown records for career punting average (40 yards per punt), season punting average (42.7 yards per punt) and single-game punting average (57 yards per punt, set in 1966 against Columbia).

Brown also had a fine quarterback laboring on its undistinguished teams of the mid-1960s: Bob Hall. In 1965 Hall set Brown records for pass completions in a game (21) and a season (135). He finished the year as the top-rated passer in the Ivy League, throwing for more than 1100 yards and seven touchdowns.

Above: *Leonard C Jardine, head coach from 1967 to 1972.*

Opposite top: *Quarterback Frank Finney shows his passing style. He led the Ivy League in passing, scoring and total offense in 1958.*

Opposite bottom left: *Center Gerald E Murphy was All-Ivy in 1967.*

Opposite bottom right: *Joseph R Randall set school records for single-game, season and career punting average in the mid-1960s.*

Opposite: *Seth Morris (44) carries for a gain against Harvard in 1975. He was part of the strong offense that gave Brown 258 points to its opponents' 168 that year.*

Above: *José Violante (9) steadies himself for a field goal attempt in a 1974 game. He is Brown's only three-time All-Ivy selection.*

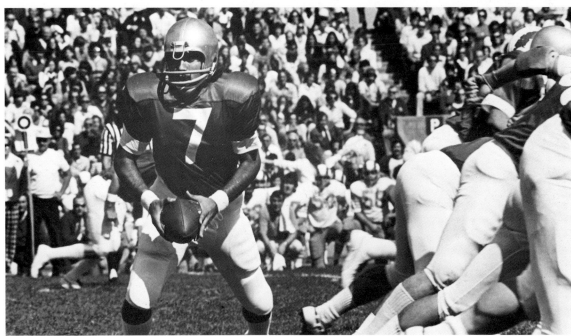

Above: *QB Pete Beatrice (7) handles the ball for the Bruins against Yale in 1973. Beatrice replaced Dennis Coleman in the second half to bring Brown a 34-25 win.*

Len Jardine relieved McLaughry as coach after the 1966 season and fared no better. His best season was a 2-6-1 campaign in 1967 that featured wins against Colgate and Columbia and a 14-14 tie at Cornell. Brown again had some individual standouts. In 1967, center Gerry Murphy, linebacker Tim Whidden and punter Dan Stewart were accorded first-team All-Ivy status.

Finally, after six consecutive losing seasons and a record of 9-44-1, Jardine was released in 1972. The Bruins brought in John Anderson, who had coached Middlebury College to an 8-0 record in 1972 and three winning seasons in four years. Anderson did not disappoint, inaugurating a new golden era for Brown football. In 11 seasons he would post a glittering record of 60 victories, 39 losses and three ties. His winning percentage of .603 was better than that of any Brown coach since Robinson's .624 mark.

Anderson was an innovative coach and an advocate of high-powered offenses. His first win at Brown was a perfect example of both.

Above: *Ruben Chapa's*
32-yard field goal, kicked
with nine seconds on the
clock, gave Brown a
13-10 victory over
Dartmouth in 1977.

During the first half of the 13 October 1973 contest against Yale, Anderson employed Dennis Coleman, a quarterback who preferred to 'roll out' of the pass pocket. In the second half, after Yale had adjusted to Coleman, Anderson sent in Pete Beatrice, a classic dropback passer who stayed in the pocket. The result was a 34-25 victory.

That initial Anderson season saw Brown also beat Princeton, Cornell and Columbia to finish at 4-3-1, the Bruins' first winning season since 1964 and only their second since 1958. There were even better things in store under Anderson. In 1974 Brown won an additional game, going 5-4 with consecutive wins over Princeton, Cornell, Harvard and Columbia to finish the season. In the Princeton victory Beatrice connected with Ken O'Keefe for a 77-yard touchdown pass, one of the longest completions in Brown history. Beatrice went on to set a Brown career passing record with 3015 yards through the air.

In 1975 Brown rode the running of Seth Morris and Kevin Slattery and the accurate passing of Bob Bateman to a 6-2-1 mark, the school's best record since 1954. Brown's potent offense outscored the opposition, 258-168, and scored more than 40 points on three occasions – against Rhode Island (41-20), Harvard (45-23) and Columbia (48-13).

One of the stars of the 1975 team, as well as the 1973 and 1974 squads, was soccer-style placekicker José Violante, Brown's only three-time All-Ivy selection. Violante kicked four field goals of 48 yards or more during his career, and at one time held the school record with his 51-yard field goal against Pennsylvania in 1975.

The fine 1975 season was just a prelude to 1976, when Brown missed its second unbeaten season by one point and captured its only Ivy League championship with an 8-1 record. Brown shared the title with Yale, which was

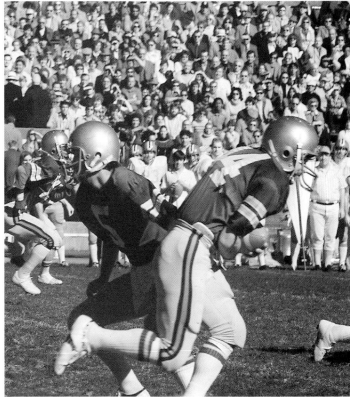

Above: *Star receiver Bob Farnham (46) returns a punt against the University of Rhode Island at Brown Stadium in 1975.*

Top right: *QB Mark Whipple (5) hands off to Seth Morris (44) in 1978.*

also 6-1 in Ivy play. The Elis' only loss was a season-opening 14-6 defeat by Brown. Brown's lone setback was a 7-6 loss to Pennsylvania. That championship Brown team was blessed with one of the Bruins' all-time great receivers in Bob Farnham, who set a career mark for receptions with 108. Farnham was named honorable mention All-American in 1976, Brown's first player to receive that designation in six seasons.

The 1976 offense broke Brown team season marks with Farnham setting two career records and quarterback Paul Michalko establishing two single-game records. Both were rewarded with first-team All-Ivy status in 1976. The defense, led by All-Ivy linebacker Scott Nelson, was just as important. It ranked among the top defenses in the nation throughout the season and was the key to early-season wins over Yale, Rhode Island (3-0) and Princeton (13-7) before the offense began its record-setting scoring.

Above: *QB Paul Michalko (4) scrambles versus Princeton.*

That was the pinnacle of Anderson's tenure, but he would go on to have very good teams for the next four years. In 1977, led by safety Ron Brown (who would go on to become an assistant coach, first at his alma mater, then at Nebraska), center Mike Knight and defensive tackle Kevin Rooney, Brown posted a 7-2 record. The two losses were close ones, coming against Ivy champ Yale (10-9) and Pennsylvania (14-7). Brown went into its season finale at Columbia with one eye on New Haven, where Yale was meeting Harvard. A win by the Crimson combined with a Brown victory would have given the Bruins a share of the Ivy crown for a second straight season. Yale would have none of that, though, taking a convincing 24-7 win, making Brown's 21-14 decision before 8500 at Brown Stadium purely academic.

One of Brown's more thrilling wins of the 1977 campaign was a 13-10 triumph against Dartmouth on a 32-yard field goal by Ruben Chapa with nine seconds to play. Chapa also set a Brown record for longest field goal during that season with a 53-yarder against Holy Cross.

Brown had a series of top quarterbacks in the 1970s. After Beatrice came Michalko and he was followed by Mark Whipple, who called the signals in 1977 and 1978 and was rated by some as the premier quarterback in the Ivy League. Whipple threw for 2365 yards during his career. In 1978, Whipple threw for 1300 of those yards to lead the Bruins to a 6-3 record that was highlighted by wins over Princeton, Harvard and Holy Cross. Against the Crim-

son, Whipple's two-point conversion pass to Rick Villella lifted Brown to a 31-30 win at Harvard Stadium.

Whipple was succeeded by Larry Carbone, who passed for nearly 2800 yards in 1979 and 1980. Carbone's aerial efficiency helped Brown post a record of 6-4 in 1980, Anderson's last winning season. Carbone set a school record when he threw for 1587 yards in 1980. One of his favorite targets was tight end Steve Jordan, who finished his Brown career in 1981 with 74 receptions. Jordan progressed to even better things with the Minnesota Vikings of the National Football League. A seventh-round draft choice by the Vikings in 1982, Jordan led the National Football Conference's tight ends in receptions in 1985 with 68 catches. Jordan left Brown trailing only the Farnham brothers – Mark and Bob – on the career receiving yardage list.

Jordan was not the only professional player of Brown vintage during this time. Linebackers John Woodring and John Prassas, both of whom completed their Brown careers in 1980, went on to play in the pro ranks, Woodring with the NFL's New York Jets and Prassas in the Canadian Football League.

Just as Carbone had done before him, Hank

Above: QB Larry Carbone (12) in action against Dartmouth in 1980. He set a school record by passing for 1587 yards that season.

Top left: QB Hank Landers (6) gets good protection from Bill Barrett (32) during a game with Princeton in 1981. In his only season of play for the Bruins he broke Larry Carbone's single-season passing record with a whopping 1913 yards.

Opposite: Tight end Steve Jordan celebrates a touchdown in 1980. He went on to play pro football for the Minnesota Vikings, where his 68 receptions in 1985 topped the NFC.

Above: *Ace running back Jamie Potkul moves the ball downfield for the Bruins in 1985.*

Top right: *The Brown bench observes the action on the gridiron in 1984.*

Right: *Defensive back Kieron Bigby (1) runs an interception back for a touchdown against Yale in 1984. On the day, he returned three interceptions for 216 yards and two touchdowns.*

Far right: *Placekicker Alex Kos (15) watches to see if a field goal attempt clears the uprights.*

Opposite: *Coach John Rosenberg has a word with his squad in 1985.*

Landers stepped in at quarterback and surpassed his predecessor's passing totals. Landers played just one season – 1981 – but he made it count by passing for a Brown-record 1913 yards on 131 completions. Taking over the quarterback spot in 1982 was Joe Potter, who threw for 2954 yards during his career to rank second only to Beatrice's career total of 3015. Potter's best year was his junior season of 1982, when he threatened Carbone's season record but fell just short with 1516 yards through the air. The Bruins were a 5-5-1 team in 1982, with their big wins coming against Yale, Cornell and William and Mary.

In 1984 John Rosenberg, a former assistant to Paterno at Penn State, replaced Anderson as Brown's sixteenth head coach. Under Rosenberg, a former Harvard player, the emphasis switched from record-setting quarterbacks to a record-setting running back, Jamie Potkul.

Rosenberg's debut came on 21 September 1984, and the Bruins presented him with a suitable gift, a 27-14 victory against Yale. The star of the day was defensive back Kieron Bigby, who in his first game with the varsity set or tied five NCAA records with three interceptions returned for 216 yards and two touchdowns. Bigby was an exceptionally versatile athlete. During his career at Brown, the 5-foot 11-inch, 180-pounder played defensive back, wide receiver and even started at quarterback.

Above: *The Brown Band takes the field during halftime festivities at the annual homecoming game.*

Far left: *Linebacker John Woodring (45) graduated in the Brown Class of 1980 and proceeded to a pro career with the New York Jets.*

Potkul, who came from Green Brook, New Jersey, made his first noise as a junior in 1984. In the final game of that season he scored three touchdowns – one of them on a 94-yard kick-off return – as Brown beat Columbia to finish at 4-5-1. As a senior in 1985 Potkul became Brown's first single-season 1000-yard rusher and its first career 2000-yard rusher. Potkul capped his career in 1985 with a 198-yard game against Columbia, giving him 1005 yards for the season. He ran for 2159 yards during his three-year career.

Sharing the spotlight with Potkul in 1985 was the outstanding placekicker, Chris Ingerslev. He kicked a school-record 31 field goals from 1983 to 1985, and when he left Brown only one player (fellow kicker José Violante) had put more points on the board in a Brown uniform. Ingerslev connected on nine straight field goals during a two-game span in 1985.

Brown's biggest upset of 1985, and indeed in quite some time, was a 32-27 triumph over Rhode Island, a team that finished the season ranked seventh in the nation in Division 1-AA. Potkul led the offense by rushing for 115 yards and sophomore Walt Cataldo helped to stop

Rhode Island's powerful passing attack with a pair of interceptions.

In 1986 Brown posted a record of 5-4-1. One of the highlights again came against Rhode Island's Rams, as Brown took a 27-7 decision, giving the Bruins their fifth win in seven years against their only in-state rival. Then in 1987 Brown got off to its best start of Rosenberg's first four seasons, with wins in four of its first five games, including a 23-15 victory over Cornell that thrust Brown briefly to the top of the Ivy League. One of the leading offensive figures on the 1987 team was Alex Kos, another in the string of fine Bruin placekickers; Kos's 22-yard field goal with 10 seconds remaining in the game against Lehigh gave Brown a 10-7 win. Then, in the season's final game, sophomore quarterback Danny Clark scored with only 47 seconds left to lead Brown to a 19-16 win over hapless Columbia.

The Bruins' fine 1987 season – 5-2 in league play, 7-3 overall – was only good enough to get them a tie with Yale for second place in the Ivy League. But there was every sign that the Brown Bruins would be back for many more seasons of solid football.

Above: *A full house at Brown Stadium watches the Bruins' performance on a sunny September afternoon in 1984.*

Top left: *Kicker Chris Ingerslev (3) receives congratulations from teammate Mark Miller following a successful field goal in 1985.*

COLUMBIA UNIVERSITY

Founded: as King's College in 1754
Location: Manhattan, New York
Undergraduate Enrollment: 5500
Colors: Columbia Blue and White
Nickname: Lions

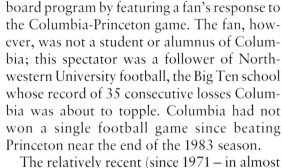

When Columbia University played Princeton on 10 October 1987, the Lions commanded more national attention than they had in 40 years, when in mid-October 1947 the Columbia football team had beaten Army in 'The Little Miracle of Baker Field.' CBS Sports had already taped an interview so that even before the game began, the network was prepared to add some color to its weekly college score-

Above: *Bill Morley, one of Columbia's early stars who helped to bring the formidable Yale team to defeat in 1899.*

Right: *Captain Smith of the 1903 Lions.*

board program by featuring a fan's response to the Columbia-Princeton game. The fan, however, was not a student or alumnus of Columbia; this spectator was a follower of Northwestern University football, the Big Ten school whose record of 35 consecutive losses Columbia was about to topple. Columbia had not won a single football game since beating Princeton near the end of the 1983 season.

The relatively recent (since 1971 – in almost 120 years of football) history of failure associated with Columbia belies a respectable, at times enviable, tradition. With no intention of being part of a feeder network for the professional leagues, Columbia has fielded more than one team of distinction; it has even graduated several All-Americans. Furthermore, among its football alumni are players who have won durable reputations playing for professional teams. There was even an undefeated team, and a team that won the Rose Bowl.

Columbia first started playing intercollegiate football in 1870, when they met Rutgers, and in 1872 they played their first Ivy League team, Yale. Columbia lost – and went on to lose all but two of their games against Ivy League teams until 1899. But it should be said that during those years Columbia actually dropped intercollegiate football from 1885 to 1888, and again from 1892 to 1898. Besides, Ivy League teams were quite formidable in those days.

Then in 1899 Columbia engaged a well-known Yale center, George Foster Stanford, as a football coach, and overnight he provided Columbia with a respectable team. Their greatest game that season was against Yale, the most imposing of the early Ivy League teams and indeed of all the nation's college teams. Columbia's stars in that game – Harold Weekes, Bill Morley, and Jim Wright – were named by Walter Camp to his All-America team. And then, as though that game hadn't been the pinnacle for Columbia, in the next season their team defeated Princeton. When Princeton recovered a Columbia fumble and ran for a touchdown, things did not look good, but thanks to the yardage piled up by Weekes (he was especially famous for his ability to leap over the linesmen) and a pass that Morley took for a touchdown, Columbia came out with a 7-6 victory.

In 1903 Columbia fielded yet another strong team, beating Cornell for the first time in their rivalry and losing only to their nemesis, Yale. But not only was that the last strong team that Columbia fielded until the 1920s – it was almost the last team Columbia ever fielded. By the early 1900s, college football had become so

rough – there were numerous fatalities every year, due largely to a lack of proper protective gear – that many colleges were seriously considering dropping their teams. There were also claims that some players were being paid. In any case, by 1905 things had become so scandalous that Columbia's faculty, supported by the alumni and administration, voted to ban the game after the season ended. Most of the other colleges simply chose to institute reforms in the playing of the game.

It was 1915 before Columbia allowed a football team to take to the field again – and take it did. That year Columbia's team was undefeated in five games; in the first and last (St Lawrence and Wesleyan, respectively) the Lions' defense did not give up a single point. T Nelson Metcalf was in his first of four years as Columbia's head coach (and only the third coach in the school's history until then), while the player who received the most accolades was Howard Miller, who kicked a school record seven field goals that season, four of them in the game against St Lawrence (also a school record).

Metcalf succeeded in reviving interest in the sport, and his final year, 1918, was almost as satisfying as his first, with only one loss to Syracuse in the last game. The nine years without a team, however, had disrupted Columbia's football plans, at least in the judgment of Percy Haughton, who accepted the position of head coach in 1923, after five years of retirement from the game.

The exalted Haughton, of Harvard coaching fame, agreed to return to coaching, according to a story in the *New York Tribune*, in response to a salary estimated at nearly $20,000. Haughton soon announced his intention of instituting a plan for a whole new structure for the sport that could be sustained indefinitely by former players who would return as part of the coaching staff. It was a plausible strategy except, to everyone's shock and dismay, Percy Haughton died in the midst of his second year after winning eight games, losing five and tying one. Paul Withington stood in for the remainder of that season (1924), leading the Lions to a 5-3-1 finish.

Haughton was denied the opportunity to make good his promise, but he did introduce a new direction which had been missing since Columbia's decision to abandon the sport. New head coach Charles F Crowley helped

Above: *Coach T Nelson Metcalf of 1915-18. Following Columbia's ban on football from 1906-14 because of its violence, Metcalf picked up a strong team in 1915 which compiled a 5-0-0 record.*

Page 38: *A scene from Columbia's 1983 season: QB Bob Conroy (10) prepares to pass.*

sustain the new momentum by compiling a 26-17-4 record from 1925 to 1929, and by the end of the 1920s the Lions had established themselves as a winning team, claiming a winning margin of 48-37-6.

Despite such relative prosperity, the new coach in 1930 left no question about his ambitions for the Lions when he proclaimed to an audience of alumni at the onset of his first year that he had no intention of losing. This was the goal set by Lou Little, who had played for the University of Pennsylvania and then gone on to coach Georgetown. In Little's inaugural season, the Light Blue lost only one game in their first seven, but that defeat was no ordinary Saturday disappointment; it was a shellacking by Dartmouth, 54-0. Little consoled his new team by announcing that he wanted the laceration to fester until next year's meeting with the Big Green. When the 1931 rematch came, the Lions were undefeated again and had held their first three opponents scoreless. Again the Dartmouth team, with almost the same roster as that of the season before, scored on the Light Blue – but only once, while many of the same Lions who had suffered the whipping in 1930 tallied 19 points. Little's strategy of remembering had worked.

Lou Little's redefinition of Columbia's foot-

Above: *Howard Miller in the kicking position that earned him a school-record seven field goals in 1915.*

Right: *Coach Charles Crowley, expounding on the finer points of the game to his first Columbia crop in the 1925 season. By the end of his term in 1929 Columbia was firmly rooted as a winning team, with a 48-37-6 record.*

ball reputation in his first five years was a stirring achievement. He came to a campus which had been conditioned to regard football games as part of the fall calendar, but hardly more; and after a 5-4 record his first season, accomplished with only a modicum of strong players, he assembled an astonishing set of numbers during the next four years. From 1931 to 1934 the Lions lost only one game each season, tied twice and won 29 games for a combined tally of 29-4-2.

Little's culminating triumph in his first five years was the 1934 Rose Bowl game. During the season the Lions had lost only to Princeton, but the reaction to Stanford's choice of Columbia as its opponent for the prestigious game was one of disbelief and outrage by writers who charged the mighty team from the West with intentions of humiliating Columbia and Eastern football by decimating a vastly inferior team. Furthermore, response to the invitation at Morningside Heights was not uniformly enthusiastic. When Coach Little announced the invitation, he emphasized that the school's faculty and alumni had not yet accepted. The prevailing sentiment among those who would make the decision was one of skepticism at best, and the reasons were not a result of academic considerations; no one on the committee had confidence that the team could play the same kind of football Stanford had played that season.

When Lions quarterback Cliff Montgomery was given the chance to speak for the team, he announced simply that they would like the opportunity to play Stanford. Montgomery's appeal was reinforced by the argument of a former quarterback who would manage the US Office of Strategic Services during World War II, 'Wild Bill' Donovan. Donovan

Top: *The Columbia football team in 1921.*

Above: *Lion halfback Lou Gehrig in 1922, who went on to baseball fame after signing with the Yankees the following year.*

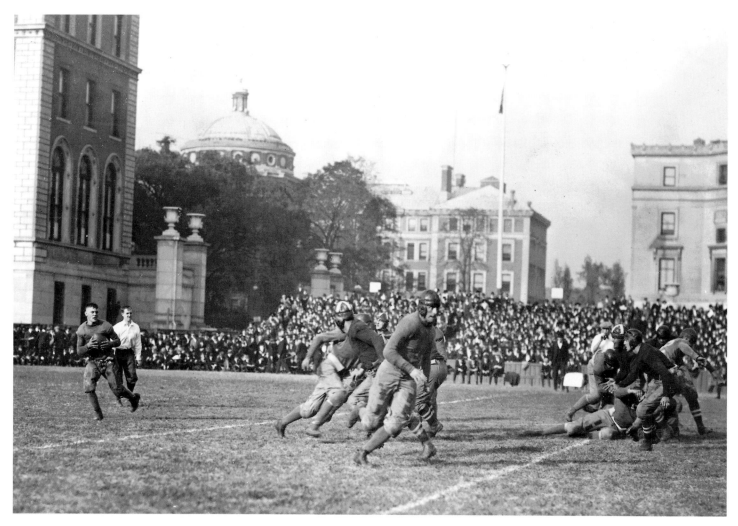

reasoned that what was to the committee a mere invitation was in fact a point of honor to the team.

The governing body voted in favor of the game and the team began to prepare. As soon as news of Columbia's decision became public, sportswriters on the West Coast were delirious in their response, describing a scenario of carnage. Typical of the predictions was a *New York Times* story by Robert F Kelley, who offered that the Lions would be devoured by Stanford, citing as reasons the obvious superiority of the Indians, but also the seductive ambience of the Rose Bowl carnival, including Hollywood nymphs, floats and all the other pageantry accompanying the occasion. Kelley wrote that Columbia could not be expected to match powerhouses like Stanford because Eastern schools had enervated the game; it no longer offered any excitement.

Lou Little, however, had no tolerance for being patronized; and he knew there could be only one plausible strategy for beating Stanford – out-think them. During practice he drilled a new play coded KF-79. Quarterback Montgomery explained later that it was actually a variation on a standard fake by the quarterback to one of the halfbacks after slipping the ball to the fullback, who would sweep

around the end of the defensive line unexpectedly. Coach Little didn't anticipate getting more than one surprise (and possibly score) from the scheme, but that one unexpected play might win the game.

Instead of inflating the Lions with hyperbole about how this game was sure to be the upset of the century, Little enabled them to fix their concentration so that they knew what they could legitimately expect from themselves; they learned how to execute that almost flawlessly. The coach had not, however, prepared them for the worst imaginable adversary: when they arrived in Los Angeles, it was raining mercilessly. The timing necessary for their stunts would not allow for a half-step miscue under any circumstances.

All the poise the Lions had mustered in practice seemed like childish bluff when they entered the stadium amidst the din of the largest football crowd they had ever seen. In reality the 40,000 fans filled only half the stadium's seats, and the weather wasn't the only reason for all the vacancies. Many fans had neither the heart nor stomach to witness what threatened to be a massacre.

The field quickly became a marsh, but proved not as treacherous as the Stanford giants who thundered through the Lions'

Opposite top: *The Lions shut out NYU 21-0 in 1923.*

Opposite bottom: *The revered Percy Haughton (center) in 1924.*

Top: *The Lions scored a point a minute in this Haverford game, ending 59-0.*

Above: *Lou Little led some of Columbia's greatest teams and fostered some of its best talent during his 27 years as head coach (1930-56).*

defense relentlessly. Despite repeated scoring threats, however, the Light Blue linebackers managed to postpone the seemingly inevitable score. Meanwhile, quarterback Montgomery, perhaps unwisely, called for KF-79 in the first quarter, but even the *coup de grâce* was ineffectual when the Indians' safety saved a touchdown with an ankle tackle at the Stanford 11-yard line.

In the second quarter, Stanford moved inside the Columbia 25-yard line and a score seemed certain, but the Indians fumbled; the Light Blue had fumbled twice already on scoring drives. Montgomery, dissatisfied with the prospect of a stalemate, decided to call for a forward pass – an intelligent but high-risk strategy in such soggy conditions. Not altogether surprised, the Stanford defense adjusted quickly but could not deny the hustling of Tony Matal who soared over the defenders and snared the pass on the 17-yard line.

Back in the huddle, the entire Columbia team knew it was time for KF-79 again, but this time the line made adjustments. Once more, the timing in the handoff from Montgomery to the backs was precise and Al Barabas pounded around the left end and raced toward the goal as he had the first time. Just when it appeared the play would be futile again, the Lions' clever right guard, McDowell, hurled himself into the Stanford safety and Barabas waltzed untouched into the end zone.

It was to be the only score of the game. In the second half Stanford played brutally, but so did the Light Blue. Stanford did not lose heart or fall apart; they played valiantly, assaulting the Columbia goal six more times in the second

half. Columbia stalled the attack each time, at times punishing the Stanford backs. The Indians' Bobby Grayson, who tallied 160 yards all alone (more than the entire Columbia backfield), finished the game with a broken rib, a fractured foot and a tribute to the Lions when he acknowledged how brutal they had been.

While the Stanford team nursed their wounds and pride, the pundits withdrew in relative silence. Only friends intimate with Lou Little had a satisfactory explanation for the Lions' conquest: it was no miracle at all, merely the result of a capable, inspired team's response to the demands of a coach who balanced perfectionism with an attitude that winning was always a possibility.

Despite the historic victory over Stanford, Columbia was unable to assemble a dominant team again until 1945 when the schedule was comparable to those arranged after 1956, with an emphasis on Ivy schools. Another performance comparable to the Rose Bowl triumph did occur, however, during the otherwise lean period from 1935 to 1945: during the 1938 season, quarterback Sid Luckman directed an un-

Opposite top: *Lion QB Cliff Montgomery kicking the ball in the 1934 Rose Bowl versus Stanford. The much-publicized underdogs, Columbia triumphed 7-0.*

Opposite middle: *(l-r) F King, C Barrett, C Montgomery, S Maroon, B Nevel, J Rissman and Coach Little with the Rose Bowl Trophy.*

Opposite bottom: *The heroes return from the Rose Bowl.*

Above: *Coach Little with Captain Montgomery.*

Right: *Back Al Barabas (left) and QB Montgomery perfected Little's fake pass play, which won the Rose Bowl for the Lions.*

heralded Lions' team in a shocking victory over Army at Michie Stadium, West Point.

When Luckman and the Lions returned for the second half, they were losing 18-6; but the savvy of Luckman and grit of the rest of the team were sufficient to stall the Cadets' offense during the second half while Columbia scored twice. Enroute to the final and winning touchdown, Luckman moved the Lions in a series of four plays from their own 20-yard mark to Army's 19, the culminating gain resulting from a 23-yard pass from Luckman to halfback Radvilas. The reception by Radvilas was costly – he was knocked unconscious, but didn't drop the ball.

Watching the game and Luckman's mastery was coach and owner of the Chicago Bears, George Halas. What impressed the judge from Chicago most was Luckman's sure hands and his ability to improvise behind an offensive line which did not provide the surest protection. Halas persuaded Luckman to play for the Bears, and the two of them began perfecting a new offensive strategy which eventually became standard in professional football – the T-formation. A quarterback playing in that position must have confident hands and be able to move adroitly both within the protective pocket and outside, where he often must scramble until he finds an open receiver. Some fans and writers who saw Luckman play ranked him as the best of his time.

College football continued to attract support during the war years, but much of the game's traditional glamor was understandably missing. Lou Little represented the prevailing mood when he declared that the competition associated with football games was being played out in a much more serious struggle commanding the attention of the entire nation and world.

Soon after the war, though, the Lions met the Cadets of Army again in another memorable contest. Coached by Red Blaik, Army had not lost in 32 games; the only other team to equal their strength in the 1947 season was the University of Pennsylvania, which played them to a 7-7 deadlock. In 'The Little Miracle of Baker Field' the Lions reawakened the dormant enthusiasm of fans everywhere, not merely followers of the Light Blue. The players for Columbia that year were among the best in the school's history; nonetheless, they were

Above: *Columbia's talented QB Gene Rossides. In the celebrated 1947 victory over Army, Rossides completed brilliant passes to Bill Swiacki and Lou Kusserow.*

Opposite top: *Halfback Lou Kusserow breaks through for the deciding TD in the 1947 battle against Army. The Cadets, who had been undefeated in 32 straight games, were upset 21-20 by the Lions.*

Opposite bottom: *The euphoric Lions, after defeating Army in 1947, boost up teammate and All-American Bill Swiacki.*

When Little retired after the 1956 season, he was among the most honored in his business, even though he had assembled a relatively undistinguished winning record with only 11 winning seasons in his 27 years at Columbia. Nor did he retire as a staunch advocate of the game of football. His own first choice as a student had been medicine, and at the age of 63 he regretted that he had not followed his original ambition to be a country doctor. He did, however, emphatically encourage every undergraduate in college to participate in interscholastic competition, but only as a way of giving something back to the school which had nurtured and prepared him academically.

Little's highest honor was bestowed by a colleague, Dean Herbert Hawkes, when he rated the coach as the school's best teacher. Little's contributions as a teacher were best summarized in his injunction to his players: hit hard enough to knock the opponent senseless, then help him get back on his feet. He loathed losing and accepting defeat; the only way to prevent continued losing, in his judgment, was to work that much harder to win the next time. Beyond a doubt Columbia University was fortunate to claim a coach like Lou Little, and Lou Little was no less fortunate to be a coach at Columbia. Typical of the school's elevated attitude toward football during the years of Little was the response from the faculty and administration to the rousing defeat of Army in 1947: more important than the 21-20 winning score was the recognition that of the 335 academic courses taken by the football Lions that year, there were only four failing grades.

The first year that Ivy League schools played each other as members of a formal league was Lou Little's last season, and Columbia won only two of seven games within league competition and tied for sixth place. New coach Buff Donelli quickly recognized that he was facing a period of reconstruction before the Light Blue would become serious contenders for a league title. He needed only five years to regain respectability for Columbia football.

Before the 1961 season opened, writers favored the Light Blue to win the Ivy League crown. Donelli could not boast an abundance of outstanding players, but he had some very good ones in quarterback Tom Vasell, a deft passer, halfbacks Tom Haggerty and Russ Warren and fullback Tom O'Connor, all of whom had proven themselves durable and able to move the football. The line was weakened by the graduation of end Bob Federspiel, but the nucleus of tackle Bob Asack (230 pounds), center Lee Black (215 pounds) and guard Bill Campbell promised enough experience to

decidedly overmatched by the Cadets. Playing quarterback for the Lions was Gene Rossides. At halfback was Lou Kusserow, who had intended to transfer to West Point after only one year at Columbia to improve his mathematics skills, but, happily for the Lions, chose rather to remain at Morningside Heights. All-American Bill Swiacki was playing end, and Ventan Yablonski was fullback.

In a stunning performance, which Blaik would later acclaim as the smartest from a Columbia quarterback in all the years he coached Army, Rossides passed for one touchdown to Swiacki and Kusserow ran for a second in the second half to recover from a 20-7 halftime deficit and defeat an Army team which had not yielded three touchdowns in a single game all season. Furthermore, Columbia's defense held the Army's vaunted attack impotent in the second half. Rossides and Kusserow, rated even today as Columbia's best backfield combination in all its 117 years of playing, thanked Coach Little for what he had done for them after the game; Little insisted that he should be thanking them.

open holes in the opposing line.

After mauling Brown (50-0) in the season opener, the Lions lost their second game to a strong Princeton team (30-20). Meanwhile Yale, last year's league champion and the next opponent for the Lions, had won its first two games and was chosen by forecasters to win the game and probably its second consecutive league title. The game was one of the most riveting of the new season and consistent with the fierce rivalry and abandoned play of Ivy League competition. In addition, the Yale game documented the coaching capabilities of Donelli, who had studied Yale's strategy and prepared the Lions, to attack the Elis at their position of strength – their running game with quarterback roll-out patterns and bruising fullback rushes through the line.

There was only one touchdown in the game, and it was scored by the Lions' sophomore fullback Al Butts, who won it by determinedly attacking the Yale line and eventually breaking through. Tom O'Connor added to the Bulldogs' misery by driving the ball through the goal posts from 23 yards for a field goal. The Lions went on to complete Donelli's most successful season at 6-1 and tied with Harvard for the league crown after the Crimson shut out Yale in the season's closing game.

The 1961 season turned out to be not only Buff Donelli's most satisfying, but the last time Columbia would finish among the league's top three for the next decade. After losing all but two of his offensive starters to graduation (guard Tony Day and fullback Tom O'Connor) and undermanned defensively, Donelli began the 1962 season with scant reason for

optimism. There was, however, one glittering new name, a sophomore quarterback who brought with him sensational credentials worthy of any football school in the country: Archie Roberts, Jr.

Roberts proceeded to make such a strong impression in his sophomore year that professional scouts shadowed him throughout his second season with the Lions. Writers and fans recognized that he was the kind of quarterback who balanced superior physical and mental abilities. Columbia fans had little reason to be enthusiastic apart from Roberts, but his performances were consistently brilliant. In the season's last two games that year, Columbia won largely because of Roberts' exceptional playing. In the 33-8 win over Penn he completed 12 of 15 passes for three touchdowns and rushed for 55 yards and one more score.

Throughout his three years playing for the Light Blue, Roberts was courted by the NFL and AFL, but he continued to insist that his aspirations were to practice medicine. In the winter after his final season at Columbia, he changed his plans somewhat and signed with Cleveland. The Browns had extended an offer of $100,000 over six years with the proviso that Roberts have the first two years to study at Western Reserve Medical School.

In 1968 Columbia appointed only its third head coach in 38 years, Frank Navarro. The new coach had the misfortune of making his entrance at Morningside Heights the same season that Marty Domres was to make his exit. Navarro rated Domres the best college quarterback he had ever watched. In his parting game the sensational Domres passed 54 times, completing 30 for 329 yards and two touchdowns. He also carried the ball for two more scores as the Lions smashed the Brown Bruins, 46-20. During his three years as quarterback for the Light Blue, Domres set 12 new Ivy League records and 15 Columbia records for passes thrown, completed passes, total passing yards gained and total offense. Furthermore he set a new NCAA standard for total offensive plays at 1132 in three years.

Even Domres, superlative as he was, could not win alone; the Lions were able to muster only two wins in Navarro's opening year. Three years later, however, the Lions and Navarro fielded Columbia's most recent team to play with authority and contend for the league title. In 1971 the Lions lost only to Harvard (21-19) and Cornell (24-21) in the league and finished with a 5-2 season in Ivy competition. It was the first time in 26 years that Columbia beat Princeton, in a fierce contest which the Tigers would have won had it not

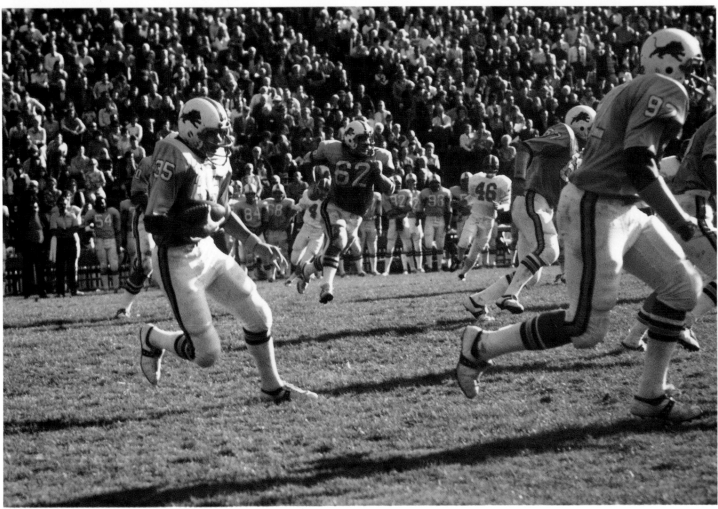

Above: Columbia's great record-setting QB Marty Domres (21), facing Brown in 1968 for his final game, completed 30 passes for 329 yards and two TDs and also ran for two TDs toward the winning score of 46-20.

Right: After lionhearted attacks on the Yale line in 1961, Columbia back Al Butts (43) finally drove through for the game's only TD. That 6-1 season was rewarded with shared first place honors with Harvard.

been for defensive back Charlie Johnson's deflecting a two-point conversion attempt in the closing seconds to avert a tie. The 1971 season was successful despite early predictions that Columbia was outclassed by opponents. The year before, some Columbia students had even called for a reassessment of the school's continuing participation in intercollegiate football.

Victories in the 1980s have come infrequently. The 1982 season was perhaps the only year to offer any consolation, despite a 1-6 record. It ended the 60-year occupancy of Baker Field, with its wooden bleachers, but it also featured the superlative play of junior quarterback John Witkowski, who set new league records for passes thrown in a single season (317), completions (166), passing yards for a season (2149) and career touchdowns (27). Witkowski's achievement was enhanced by stellar performances of juniors Bill Regio and Don Lewis, who set Ivy League records for pass receptions in a single season.

Otherwise, the first seven seasons of the 1980s have been undeniably bleak. Columbia ended the 1987 season with no wins or ties and extended its losing streak to 41. There was a disclosure in November 1987 that Columbia

Top: *Columbia QB John Witkowski (18) scrambles in the Princeton game, 8 October 1983, which the Tigers won 35-26. Witkowski accumulated new Ivy records for the season.*

Above: *Columbia's head coach, Frank Navarro, succeeded Buff Donelli in 1968.*

had exercised a waiver option provided by the Ivy League to relax academic standards for freshman football candidates. Under a league ruling, Columbia had been permitted to admit students scoring below an admissions standard set in the 1980s, a standard determined by an index comprised of Scholastic Aptitude Test scores, high school class rank and achievement test scores. A Columbia administrator explained that the variance was intended to accommodate any student demonstrating unusual ability or talent (including promise in the arts) not measureable by standardized tests, and had certainly been allowed by other Ivy League colleges. The day after the revelation that 11 freshman football players had been admitted over the 1986-87 seasons, students became embroiled in the controversy. Many reacted zealously with grave misgivings. How could an institution with 41 Nobel Prize winners on the faculty adjust academic standards to rejuvenate a faltering football program? Notwithstanding the debate, the freshman team of 1987 completed its first undefeated season in the history of Columbia football and its first winning record in 13 years. The final chapter of football at Columbia was by no means written.

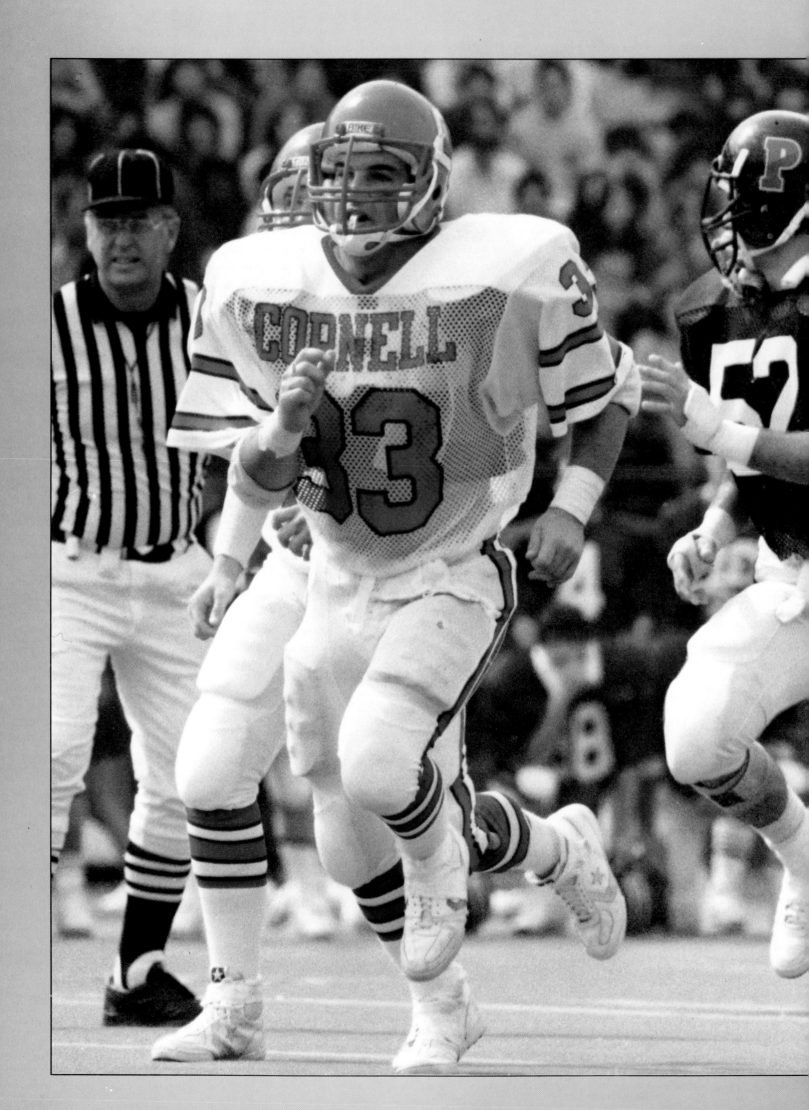

CORNELL UNIVERSITY

Founded: 1865
Location: Ithaca, New York
Undergraduate Enrollment: 12,600
Colors: Carnelian Red and White
Nickname: Big Red

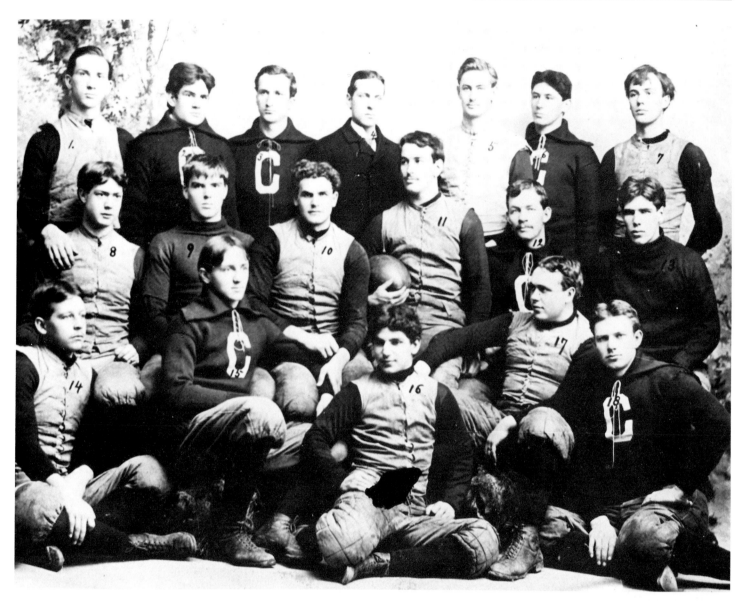

Previous pages: *Big Red's Jeff Johnson (33) during the 1985 game between Cornell and Penn.*

Above: *Cornell's varsity team in 1893. Sitting in the middle row, third from the left, is Glenn 'Pop' Warner who went on to become one of the giants in early football coaching.*

Right : *The first official Cornell football team, in 1887. In the late 1870s informal frosh-soph games at Cornell were known particularly for their anarchic 'civil war' tendencies, which kept other college teams away for awhile.*

Above: *Glenn 'Pop' Warner in 1894 at Cornell, where he played football and attained a law degree. He coached at his alma mater from 1897-98 and 1904-06. With the exceptions of Walter Camp and Amos Alonzo Stagg, no one contributed as many innovations to football as Warner. The single and double wingback formations, the crouch start and the screen pass are a few of his inventions.*

ball got wedged in a dense "scrummage" of the contending parties, and while some went in boldly to extricate it, many more would stand round looking on and naively clap their hands for joy.'

Cornell President Andrew D White was also less than favorably impressed with his boys' pioneering athletic prowess. White nixed a plan to play a game in Cleveland against Michigan in 1874 because, 'I refuse to let 40 of our boys travel 400 miles merely to agitate a bag of wind.' The administration was not the only impediment to Cornell's official entry into the record books. In the late 1870s, when Harvard and Yale were attempting to organize rules for the game, Cornell's boys insisted on their own game, a combination of soccer, rugby and anarchy so individual that no one else could, or would, play with them. It was perhaps this lack of opportunity for intercollegiate games which drove the students to acquiesce and produced its first official entry into the record books. In 1887, Cornell played Union and Lehigh, and lost both games.

Percy Field was inaugurated in 1889 in a smashing game: Cornell defeated Rochester, 124-0. That season also saw two defeats for Cornell at the hands of Yale, but a Big Red shutout of Columbia, 20-0. Cornell didn't have a regular coach until 1894, when Marshall Newell saw the school through some middling seasons. The first of the great Cornell coaches didn't come on the scene until 1897, when Glenn (Pop) Warner '94 was asked back to coach.

Elected to the National Football Hall of Fame in 1951, Warner coached the 1897 and 1898 seasons, and again from 1904 to 1906. He is compared with the legendary Amos Alonzo Stagg in his contributions to football: Warner invented several plays, including the open unbalanced formation, the crouch start, screen pass and the shifting defense. He might be most fondly remembered for his spirited hidden-ball play, first used in 1897 against Penn. Allen E Whiting, team captain in 1898, recalled how the quarterback would shove the ball up his elastic-bound jersey. While he ran for the goal line, a teammate followed to extract the ball and touch it down. But, apparently, more was required of the Big Red than the hidden ball play to beat the Quakers in 1897: Cornell lost the game, 12-6. It was their second loss in an otherwise winning season of 10-2.

Cornell had no trouble keeping archrival and neighbor Colgate in its place in those early years. From the first meeting in 1896 until Warner returned in 1904, Colgate scored only

Cornell University, sitting 'high above Cayuga's waters' in upstate New York, has always prided itself on the balance it has been able to strike between the achievements of its students and the feats of its football team, the 'Big Red.' The first football game at Cornell is not found in the record books. The intramural contest of 1869, which featured 40 men per side, resembled something 'between soccer and civil war,' according to Cornell historian Morris Bishop. In fact, although Cornell football officially took off in 1887, there were several games, or melees, prior to that. In 1870, for example, 80 sophomores and 80 freshmen fought until dark with time-outs called only for the referee to blow up the ball. Distinguished British sportsman and MP Thomas Hughes (and author of *Tom Brown's School Days*) watched a game organized for his benefit in October 1870 with elm trees used as goal posts. Hughes commented, 'Occasionally the five points against Cornell, in one game in 1898 – this despite the fearsome 'dust formation' which Colgate would use against Cornell. As recalled by one Big Red player, the only defense against the dust formation in the three-point stance was to 'pray for rain.' Such was the spirit of the game in the early days of inter-collegiate football. The dust formation notwithstanding, Colgate would not defeat Cornell until 1912, with a score of 13-7.

These early years of Big Red football contributed four of Cornell's representatives in the Football Hall of Fame: coaches Warner, Marshall Newell (1894-95) and Percy Haughton (1899-1900), and one player, All-American quarterback Clinton Wyckoff (1895 and 1896). Haughton, who spent much of his career at Harvard, led the Big Red through two winning seasons, 7-3 and 10-2. Quarterback Wyckoff was described as 'the sparkplug of the team' by one of his teammates.

From the 1890s until 1909, Cornell continued to have winning teams. In 1901, the Big Red was 11-1, losing only to Princeton. They were 8-3 in 1902. Halfback Raymond Starbuck, guards William Warner and Sanford Hunt were all named to the All-America teams of the period. Starbuck '01 and Warner '03 each took turns at coaching (Warner was Pop's younger brother). In the 1907 and 1908 seasons, Henry 'Heinie' Schoellkopf '02 took the Big Red through the last of its big years until Al Sharpe came on the scene in 1912. Schoellkopf, called 'the gentle giant' by teammates, would later be honored in the naming of Schoellkopf Field in 1915.

It took Al Sharpe one year to bring the Big Red around. In 1913, Cornell's jubilation at its second win over Penn in 20 years almost sparked riots. The 1914 team, with an overall 8-2 season, was only a hint of what would come. Team captain John O'Hearn '15, later elected to the Football Hall of Fame, was a tough defensive player. Named to the All-America team in 1914, O'Hearn was called the 'fiercest interference buster' in Cornell history. One nice bonus of the 1914 season was a 24-12 win over Penn. The next time the Big Red and the Quakers clashed, it would bring down the curtain on one of the greatest seasons in Big Red football history.

Opposite: Cornell's Gilmour Dobie, nicknamed 'Gloomy Gil,' coached from 1920 to 1955. His dour disposition goaded his team on to three triumphant 8-0 seasons from 1921 to 1923. Dobie's tactics used the off-tackle maneuver and the single-wing formation, a combination that, when perfectly timed, could produce the effect of a steamroller.

Far left: Clinton Wyckoff, an outstanding Cornell QB, was All-American in 1895 and 1896.

Below left: Henry 'Heinie' Schoellkopf '02, after whom Cornell's field was named in 1915, was the 'gentle giant' who led the Big Red's successes in the 1907 and 1908 seasons.

Below: John O'Hearn, team captain and All-American in 1914.

The year was 1915, Al Sharpe's fourth season at Cornell. As head coach, Sharpe is remembered for his versatility and his ability to inspire the will to win. That will took Cornell all the way in 1915. Undefeated through all nine games, the Big Red were named National Champions by Walter Camp. They brought the Harvard Crimson to their knees, ending Harvard's four-year winning streak with a shutout, 10-0. It was a stunning game. The lone touchdown was made on a recovered fumble by Murray Shelton, followed four minutes later by Charley Barrett's scoring plunge. Barrett was soon sidelined by an injury, forcing the captain to spend most of the game watching as helmetless Gib Cool, punter Fritz Shaverick and end Shelton kept Harvard scoreless. The final points were made on an angle kick by Shaverick. Both Barrett and Shelton were elected to the Football Hall of Fame in 1958 and 1973 respectively.

The intervening years between 1915 and the advent of Coach Gilmour Dobie were quiet. In 1918, because of the war, Cornell fielded no teams at all. The 1917 and 1919 teams had disappointing 3-6 records; in both years, Colgate and Penn shut out Cornell. Then, in 1920, a dour Scotsman named Gil Dobie came to town. Dobie brought with him a zealot's pessi-

mism, a sharp tongue, and a winning record: In his nine seasons with the Washington (State) Huskies, he had compiled a 58-0-3 record. It didn't take long for him to earn the nickname 'Gloomy Gil' at Cornell.

In his first year, Dobie brought the school record back to its pre-1916 level of 6-2. For the next three seasons, Cornell did not know defeat. Through the years 1921, 1922 and 1923, Cornell scored 1051 points while holding the opposition to 81. It was three years of 8-0 seasons. The Big Red pantheon of the time consisted of quarterback George Pfann '24, halfback Eddie Kaw '23 and tackle Frank 'Sunny' Sundstrom '24, all of whom have places in the Football Hall of Fame, as well as such notables as Leonard 'Swede' Hanson, Floyd Ramsey and Charley Cassidy '25. For Coach Dobie, though, there were no stars, only grunts on the battlefield.

Dobie's strategy relied on the off-tackle maneuver and the single-wing formation. Both required perfect timing. George Pfann '24 later wrote that Dobie needed 'two tandem guards who could swing out behind the line in lockstep at full speed and block effectively downfield as interference. On defense, these same guards had to be able to charge and tackle.' Pfann summed up Dobie's strategy as a combi-

Top left: *Guard Bill Warner, Pop Warner's younger brother, captained the Big Red team to an 8-3 season in 1902 and became head coach the following year.*

Above: *Al Sharpe, coach from 1912 to 1917, regularly inspired his players to win: for example, they won all nine games in 1915, breaking Harvard's four-year winning streak with a 10-0 shutout.*

Opposite top: *Cornell halfback Eddie Kaw swings around the left end for ten yards in the 1921 game against Dartmouth. Cornell won 59-7.*

Opposite bottom: *The 1922 Big Red National Champions. Front row, beginning second from left, is the core of the team: tackle Frank Sundstrom, QB George Pfann, halfback Eddie Kaw, halfback Floyd Ramsay, and fullback Charley Cassidy.*

With the end of the 1923 season and the inevitable departure of the stars of the backfield, the Big Red fell on trying times. The team won only four games in 1924, losing to Williams and Dartmouth and shut out by Penn and Rutgers. In 1925 Penn again held Cornell scoreless while Dartmouth smashed them, 62-13, for a 6-2 overall. On campus, while the Athletic Association had replaced the east stands at Schoellkopf Field with the great concrete Crescent (seating capacity 21,500) there was a continuing debate between alumni who wanted talented players recruited to the school and the faculty/administration refusal to yield to that pressure. At Cornell, the emphasis on sports was for healthy bodies to accompany healthy minds, not to field winning football teams. Additionally, there was a change in student orientation – the gala cheering crowds of pre-war times had dwindled, rallies were poorly attended and organized cheering was almost a thing of the past.

In this atmosphere, and with only respectable seasons, Gloomy Gil's fortunes dwindled. Tolerance also dwindled for his refusal to

nation of power with timing and 'a little passing and deception to keep [the other side] off balance.' Dobie employed a seven-man line and box defense 'so carefully worked out there was no formation that we saw in football which his general system of defense did not fit.'

The effect of Dobie's Cornell elevens was similar to that of a steamroller. In three games against Penn, the steamroller shut them out twice and allowed only one touchdown in 1923. In 1921, the Big Red ran up 110 points against scoreless Western Reserve. This was the game during which star halfback Eddie Kaw got the bench for breaking away for a 65-yard touchdown with Cornell leading by 100. 'When you play for me you follow your interference. It's out there for a purpose,' said Dobie. Kaw, All-American in 1921 and 1922, was characterized as a 'cocky individual' by teammate George Pfann, but one who could always produce under pressure. Kaw's running style made him unstoppable. He ran with short steps and high knee action which gave him a 'twisting, halting manner' that allowed him to slip away from tacklers.

In 1923, both Cornell and Yale lay claim to the National Championship with 8-0-0 records. The two teams did not play each other, and would not meet until 1936. Among other memories of the era was the Rose Bowl invitation of 1921, nixed by school officials concerned about over-emphasis of athletics on a campus where learning was paramount.

Above: *The Cornell-Ohio State game of 1939, which gave Cornell its 18th victory in its winning streak.*

Left: *Toward the end of Dobie's term Cornell's record dipped to a winless season in 1935. Shown here is Carl Snavely, who pulled the team's record back up to 19-3-1 for the 1938-40 seasons.*

allow students or alumni to attend practice, for his boarding up of the Field House windows to keep out spies, and for his wounding sarcasms. Although there were still good seasons – in 1931 team captain and end José C Martinez-Zorilla '31 was named All-American while the Big Red made it 7-1 – Dobie's time was coming to an end. In addition to his personality, he was criticized for not being innovative and for not keeping up with changes in the game such as the new uses of the forward pass. Dobie blamed his material. In 1935 he hit bottom with Cornell's only winless season since 1887, 0-6-1. He resigned under pressure and moved on to Boston College. Dobie was elected to the National Football Hall of Fame in 1951. In 33 years of coaching, nearly half, 14 seasons in all, were undefeated seasons for Coach Gilmour Dobie. At Cornell for 16 years, his record was 82-36-7.

Cornell football would not stay in the cellar long, especially with Coach Carl Snavely at the helm. In 1936, Snavely left North Carolina for Cornell; he brought with him 20 years of experience coaching at Bucknell and Carolina, high standards, and a genial personality. In his first year he pulled his team up to 3-5, with an honorable mention for rising star Jerome 'Brud' Holland. In 1937 and 1938, Holland was named All-America end for his swift running and terrorizing defense. Holland had tremendous running ability, as shown in his execution of Snavely's end around reverse. His

Top: *Cornell's QB George Pfann attempting to break past Dartmouth's left tackle in the 29 October 1921 game played in Troy, NY.*

Above: *Cornell captain and end José C Martinez-Zorilla was named All-American in 1932.*

Left: *Frank 'Sunny' Sundstrom '24, power tackle for the Big Red in 1923.*

defensive play kept Yale's Clint Frank in check and held Yale to a 9-0 game in 1937. This kind of playing earned Holland national recognition, by then unusual for an Ivy League player. Holland and his coach were elected together to the National Football Hall of Fame in 1965.

The Cornell eleven lost only to Syracuse and Yale, and tied Dartmouth for a 5-2-1 season in 1937. In 1938, the Big Red lost to Syracuse by two points and tied Penn in a 0-0 game. The teams of 1938, 1939 and 1940 are the stuff of great football stories. They were winners and, under the leadership of Snavely, whom they called the Gray Fox, they learned how to be good losers. Their record for the three years before World War II was 19-3-1 which included an 18-game winning streak that lasted through an upset of the brawny Ohio State Buckeyes and ended in 1940 at the infamous fifth-down play in Hanover. Certainly, Dobie's teams of the 1920s had a better overall record, but Snavely's teams had drama.

The teams were whipped into shape by Doc Kavanagh, the trainer famous for his promotion of gelatin for energy and bicycles for leg muscles (single-speed bikes are tough going up Ithaca's hills). Kavanagh also encouraged competition, and allowed enough horseplay to make calisthenics endurable. In 1939, Snavely's team was fit and far from fat: Mort Lansberg '41, who started in 1939 as a fullback replacing injured Vince Eichler, only weighed 169 pounds. Fred West was the biggest man on the team at 6-foot 3-inches and 223 pounds. Most of the team weighed in at around 170

Opposite top: *Cornell right halfback Whit Baker (53) outruns his Princeton pursuers, making 87 yards and a second TD on 14 October 1939. A few minutes earlier Baker had made a 25-yard run. The afternoon ended with a 20-7 upset by the Big Red.*

Opposite bottom: *Another Cornell halfback, Hal McCullough, pictured here in 1939.*

pounds. Sportswriter Allison Danzig '21 called it a team of speed and brains rather than brawn and power: 'It strikes for its touchdowns in the manner of Knute Rockne teams of old, going all the way with a single long gainer behind perfect blocking downfield, or a short succession of beautifully executed plays, rather than crunching out touchdowns with a string of first downs. It is one of the most accomplished teams in the use of the forward pass.'

The perfect year, 1939, began with wins over Syracuse and Princeton. The Big Red shut out Penn, 47-0, and then packed their bags for Columbus, Ohio where they would meet the Buckeyes of Ohio State. The Big Red might never have been better prepared for any game. Snavely and his staff knew by heart all of the formations the Buckeyes would use to roll down the field. The Big Red intended to hold OSU like no team had ever done before. In fact, Cornell was held scoreless well into the second quarter. The Buckeyes had two touchdowns on 86- and 72-yard drives. It looked like the Western Conference giants might take the game when, behind perfect blackout blocking, Walter 'Pop' Scholl '41 raced 79 yards off tackle for Cornell's first touchdown. For the second, Scholl passed 26 yards to Swifty Bohrman '41, who took it another 37 for the score. Hal McCullough '41 made it three with All-American tackle Nick Drahos '41 kicking the 27-yard field goal. The final score: 23-14. A stunning upset, and the first such in Cornell history.

The Big Red, plagued with injuries and exams, almost gave Colgate a tie, but Colgate's last-minute field goal failed and the 1939 season just kept on going: Cornell 14, Colgate 12. The following Saturday, the Indians at Hanover were fighting mad at the team which had spoiled their winning streak last year. Cornell with its agility, speed and passing ability never gave Dartmouth a chance: 35-6. And finally, Cornell did to Penn what Yale, Har-

vard and Navy had failed to do: The Big Red squashed the Quakers, 26-0. Snavely called it a perfect game. It crowned a perfect season with a Lambert Trophy, fourth place in the nation and rumors of a bid for the Rose Bowl. Again, Bowl games were not part of the program at Cornell. If there was an invitation, or the possibility of one, it was quashed by an administration that did not want to further strain the scholastic pursuits of its football players.

In 1940, with Walt Matuszak captain, the Big Red continued its streak, shutting out Col-

Above: *The famous 'fifth down' play in the 19 November 1940 game against Dartmouth. After the fourth down, the scoreboard read only a third down. The confused referee gave Cornell another shot. Here, with six seconds left, Scholl completes a pass to Murphy in the end zone.*

Below: *Cornell tackle Nick Drahos in 1939.*

gate and Army and allowing Syracuse one touchdown, 33-6. The Buckeyes came to town, still blinking, and Cornell took them out, 21-7, and then shut out Columbia and Yale. Up in Hanover, it was Coach Earl Blaik's last season, and the Indians were psyched. Through the first half, the Big Red could not even get past its own 40-yard line. Dartmouth, with three points on the scoreboard, held Cornell scoreless down to the last four-and-a-half minutes of play. With an 18-game streak at risk, Cornell battled down to the Dartmouth 5. With a first down and 60 seconds remaining on the clock, Coach Snavely called a time out, stopping the clock with the ball two feet from the goal line. A five-yard penalty on Cornell for delaying the game sent the ball back to the Dartmouth six. On the fourth down, Scholl's pass to Murphy was batted down, but the referee became confused: The scoreboard indicated a third down. The ball was given back to Cornell, and with six seconds left, Scholl hit Murphy in the end zone. Drahos converted for the final score of 7-3.

In their dressing room, the Indians were on the warpath. On Monday, back in Ithaca, Snavely and his staff reviewed the films. There was no doubt – Cornell had made its winning touchdown on a fifth down. Snavely and athletic director Jim Lynah conceded the defeat in telegrams to Dartmouth and offered their congratulations to the 'gallant Dartmouth team.' It's been called one of the greatest renunciations in the history of sport.

Although they gave it their best effort, Cornell was unable to stop Penn and the Quakers took the last game of 1940, 22-20. Tackle Nick

Top: *Coach Tom Harp with 1961 Cornell players (l-r): Carm DiGiacomo, Roland Marion, QB Gary Wood, Marcello Tino, John McCarthy and Pete Gogolak.*

Above: *Jack Musick, coach from 1966-74.*

Left: *In a scene from the most exciting game of 1951, Cornell's Reginald Marchant (35), Jack Dorrance (28), and Russell MacLeod (67) come in for a kill against Michigan. The Big Red had never gone to the Rose Bowl before and savored their 20-7 win over the Wolverines, former Bowl champions.*

Drahos had his second year as an All-America selection. (Drahos was also elected to the National Football Hall of Fame in 1981.) Cornell had a 5-3 season in 1941, defeating Syracuse, Harvard, Colgate, Yale and Dartmouth.

In the first of the war seasons, 1942, Cornell won only three games, defeating Lafayette, Yale and Dartmouth. In the second year, with the Navy and Marine V-12 programs in effect, colleges became stations for enlistees assigned to them by the Navy Personnel Office. So it was that Snavely found himself coaching the captain of the pre-war Penn team and enduring a reshuffling of his entire team at the end of each academic term. In 1943, 'Cornell' won 6 of 10 games, including a shutout of Dartmouth which was played at Boston's Fenway Park.

Snavely left Cornell after the war to return to North Carolina. In 1947, after a couple of middling seasons, George 'Lefty' James took over as head coach. In his first year, Cornell won only four games. James' championship crop bore fruit in 1948 when Cornell lost only to Army and yanked the Ivy championship away from Penn. Among the stars of the 1948 championship season were Hillary Chollet '50 and Pete Dorset '50. Chollet was the team's leading pass receiver in 1948. Dorset, twice a

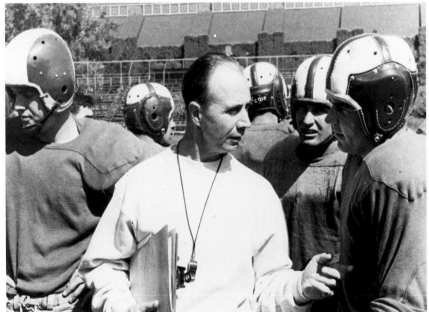

Above: *In 1947 George 'Lefty' James took over the Cornell squad after Snavely left.*

Purple Heart in the War, proved his valor again when he played a 1949 game against Penn with a broken nose. At the half, Cornell was losing, 21-7, when quarterback Dorset drove in victory touchdowns for a final of 29-21. Cornell basked in another championship year in 1949, losing only to Dartmouth.

Cornell had won 23 of 27 games in the last three years, but faced the new decade with the

loss of 15 graduating seniors. One of the major games of the 1950 season was played on a 'marsh' in 65-mph winds in Philadelphia against Penn. It was a freak hurricane that scoured the field and made passing almost impossible. Fullbacks Jeff Fleischmann '51 and Hal Seidenberg '52 mopped up the mudbath with a score of 13-6. For the season, Cornell went 4-2-0 against the Ivies, losing to Princeton (27-0) and Columbia (20-19).

The most exciting game of 1951 pitted the Wolverines of Michigan against the Big Red. The match-up with the former Rose Bowl champs brought out 35,300 fans to Schoellkopf Field. The Big Red, who had never been allowed to a Bowl game, made the most of this opportunity by smashing the Wolverines, 20-7. Cornell pulled off a 6-3 season, losing only to Princeton, Columbia and Penn, but Coach James lost 24 seniors at the end of that 1951 season. For the next six years, Cornell would fare middle-to-poor. In 1956, the official beginning of the Ivy League, Cornell won only one game – against the Quakers, 20-7.

There was a rally in 1958 – Cornell was 6-3, losing only to Syracuse, Brown and Dartmouth, and tying Princeton for number two in the Ivy League. In James' last season for Cornell, 1960, the Big Red defeated his alma mater Bucknell and shut out Harvard; but at 2-7 for the season, Cornell tied Brown for the bottom of the Ivy League.

In December 1960, Cornell hired Tom Harp from Army to replace James. At 33, Harp was the youngest head coach in the league. The Big Red stayed in the middle of the league throughout Harp's five years, enjoying only one winning season: in 1963 they were 5-4, defeating Lehigh, Yale, Columbia, Brown and Penn. The early 1960s, though, were the days of expert placekicker Pete Gogolak '64 and quarterback Gary Wood '64, the team's rushing leader. Gogolak's soccer-style conversion kicking was outstanding: in three years he missed only one point, scoring 54 of 55 PATs. His early plans to become a dentist were renounced in favor of a pro career with the Buffalo Bills. Wood was also snapped up by the Bills. An outstanding

Above: *Ed Marinaro grapples the ball as Princeton Tigers bring him down in 1970. Cornell squeezed past the Tigers 6-3.*

Top right: *Sandwiched between the Musick and Blackman years, Coach George Seifert's short term (1975-76) found Cornell in the Ivy cellar.*

Opposite: *All-Ivy tackle Steve Duca (97) alongside a Big Red teammate.*

quarterback, his many records would be broken only by the great Ed Marinaro. In passing, Wood was tops from 1961 to 1963 with a total of 1891 yards and 18 touchdowns. His career total for touchdowns was 37, 19 of them rushing. Only Marinaro would do better, with 52 touchdowns for Cornell, all by rushing. Coach Harp left Cornell for Duke after the 1965 season. Despite his stars, he left a five-year record of 19-23-3.

Cornell hired away Jack Musick from Dartmouth where he had been Bob Blackman's chief assistant as head line coach and defense specialist for the last 11 years. In Musick's first season at Cornell, 1966, the Big Red was 6-3 overall, 4-3 and fourth place in the league. Musick saw Dartmouth in town for the fiftieth rematch and a trouncing of Cornell, 32-23. In the 16-14 homecoming victory against Yale, offensive halfback Pete Larson '67 set an Ivy record by returning a kickoff 99 yards for a touchdown, with valuable blocking from Chris Ritter '69. In 1967, Cornell defeated two

of the three Ivy defending champs when they downed Princeton, 47-13, and Dartmouth, 24-21. Only Harvard and Yale defeated Cornell, which tied 14-14 against Brown. The 6-2-1 overall season put Cornell at third place in the league.

In 1969, Ed Marinaro started setting records as a sophomore on the varsity team. Although 1969 was a losing season for Cornell, 4-5 overall, the Big Red improved steadily to peak in Marinaro's senior year and tie for first place in the league. Marinaro put Cornell back on the All-America teams in 1970 and 1971; he also made touchdowns and set records — lots of them. In three years of rushing, the tailback set a record of 4715 yards with a career game average of 174.6, also a record. Marinaro established eight NCAA career records and tied another, six NCAA single-season records and three other NCAA records. He holds 12 Ivy records in rushing yardage, carries, touchdowns and points scored. In his career at Cornell, he scored 36 touchdowns for 224 points in Ivy games. His best Ivy game rushing was in 1969 against Harvard when he went for 281 yards, scoring five touchdowns. Cornell took that game, 41-24. Marinaro was awarded so many prizes and honors in his three years that it came as quite a blow when he was not awarded the Heisman Trophy: he was a close second to Auburn's Pat Sullivan in 1971. People in Ithaca actually cried when they heard the news.

Along with Marinaro's records came a winning personality. His coaches and teammates respected him because he worked hard. Marinaro was diligent about practice, weightlifting and wind sprints; he was also funny, kind and humble. After Cornell, Marinaro went on to the Minnesota Vikings and later to television for awhile as a policeman on *Hill Street Blues*.

With Marinaro and his mates' departure from the team, Cornell's fortunes again lapsed.

Opposite: *Tom Aug (8) kicked three field goals during Cornell's smashing 15-0 victory over Yale in 1986. His total of nine field goals set a new single-season record.*

Left: *Jeff DeLamielleure (46) making a clean hit in a game against Brown in 1986. In the same season he was honored as Ivy Player of the Week for his two interceptions in the Yale game.*

Bottom left: *DE Tom McHale pauses between plays in 1987.*

Below: *The bright Big Red band strikes up some pep during halftime at the Penn game in 1986.*

Above: *Coach Maxie Baughan after the final game of the 1986 season in which Cornell made a valiant defensive effort against Penn, who retained the championship.*

Opposite: *Running back Jeff Johnson (33) does some classic scrambling in 1986. In the season-opener against Princeton Johnson ran a memorable 81 yards in a 94-yard TD drive.*

1982 that Cornell had players again on the All-Ivy football first team: tight end Dan Suren '83, tailback Derrick Harmon '84, tackle Steve Duca '83 and halfback Scott Walter '83 all made the team. The four-game winning streak at the end of the 10-game 1982 season was the longest winning streak since the seven-in-a-row of 1971. Blackman left at the end of the 1982 season, and was replaced by Maxie Baughan.

After three losing seasons under Baughan, the Cornell eleven again hit the big time in 1986. The only Ivy defeat that year came at the hands of Penn, 31-21. Defensive end Tom McHale '87 took All-America honors, and the Big Red was ranked fifteenth in the NCAA Division I-AA, second in the Ivies. The season began with a confident defeat of Princeton, 39-8. It was the first time Cornell had won its opener since 1980. The defense forced four turnovers and took three directly to score, and running back Jeff Johnson took an 81-yard run on a 94-yard touchdown drive in the third quarter. Cornell then defeated Colgate for the first time since 1979 with a score of 21-12. The 33-22 loss at Lafayette toughened the Big Red resolve to win – something they would need against Harvard.

In Cambridge, Cornell fought hard for a 3-0 victory, its first in Crimsonland since 1978. The defense was superb as it held Harvard to two first downs and 43 yards in the first half. Brown, Dartmouth and Bucknell fell, setting the stage for a triumphant homecoming win over Yale, 15-0. Jeff DeLamielleure was honored as Ivy Player of the Week for his two interceptions, and Tom Aug's three field goals made a single-season record for field goals with nine, surpassing the old mark of eight by John Killian '70 and Ron Reja '80. After the 28-0 shutout over Columbia, the Big Red was ready for its final and biggest showdown of the season. Schoellkopf Stadium was filled with the largest crowd since the Marinaro days to see the Cornell eleven take on defending champs, the Quakers of Pennsylvania. 'We played our hearts out,' summed it up for senior defensive end Tom McHale. The Quakers held on to their 10-point lead despite all the efforts of the Big Red, but the Cornell eleven, who allowed only 103 points in 10 games, won a number one ranking in the East for defensive superiority.

In Musick's remaining three years at Cornell, only 1972 was a winning season, 6-3. Cornell and Penn shared third place in the league. In 1973 and 1974, Cornell was at sixth and seventh place in the league, respectively.

Cornell replaced Musick with George Seifert from the Pacific-8 in 1975; that year Cornell was beaten by everyone except Bucknell. In 1976, Cornell took two Ivy games, defeating Harvard and Pennsylvania, for a four-way tie at the bottom of the league. Seifert left after the 1976 season to be replaced by Bob Blackman, most recently of the 'Fighting Illini' at the University of Illinois. Even with a coach of Blackman's skill – his tenure at Dartmouth and Illinois would qualify him for election to the National Football Hall of Fame in 1987 – the Big Red could not get themselves up to another championship season. In fact, it wasn't until

Coach Baughan lost 10 All-Ivy seniors with the end of the 1986 season. His 1987 team had a 5-5 season overall, tying at fourth place in the Ivies with Princeton with a 4-3 record. But Cornell fans know a championship year can always be just around the corner.

DARTMOUTH COLLEGE

Founded: 1770
Location: Hanover, New Hampshire
Undergraduate Enrollment: 4000
Colors: Dartmouth Green and White
Nickname: Big Green

Top: *The 1901 team confirmed the beginning of the Dartmouth Green's winning tradition.*

Left: *Walter McCornack coached Dartmouth to a rank amongst the nation's top ten in 1902.*

Above: *The first championship team in 1893 practicing under coach Wallace Moyle.*

Dartmouth College, in Hanover, New Hampshire, is particularly noted for its winter sports, and perhaps the weather had something to do with it but it is a fact that football had to struggle to be born at Dartmouth. College authorities insisted the first goal post, put up in 1876 by John Ingham '77, Lewis Parkhurst '78 and Chalmers Stephens '77, be taken down. In 1878, students were interested in the new game, but stumped; the rules were too complicated. When school authorities finally decided to field the first team, in 1880, the players had to borrow uniforms from Princeton. The players were further handicapped because they were campused – the faculty would not allow play outside of Hanover. Finally, in 1881, Amherst allowed its boys to venture to the North Country and play the then-called Indians. Amherst lost the first and tied the second game, 1-0 and 0-0.

Football nearly met an early death in Hanover as a result of a traumatic trouncing by the Crimson tide in 1882. Reflecting on the 53-0 score *The Dartmouth*, in an editorial, stated morosely, 'It is our sad duty to conduct the melancholy obsequies . . . There was no doubt, no mystery about its death, and an inquest is totally unnecessary . . . Now, if there is any other game that Dartmouth can play better than 'foot-ball' it would be well to encourage it.'

Of course, that was not the end of Dartmouth 'foot-ball'. In fact, Dartmouth has had the best record in the Ivies, with 13 Ivy Championships, 7 their own and 6 shared, plus 2 Lambert Trophies. In 106 years of play, Dartmouth has contributed 11 men to professional football, 50 to All-America teams, and 17 to All-Ivy teams. Five coaches are in the National Football Hall of Fame, along with six players. Dartmouth, too, was the school that abandoned its symbol of the Indian as school mascot. In 1968, at the impetus of Howard Bad Hand '72, and others, the school put away all references to its Indian symbol and mascot, accepting the idea that they were perpetuating an unrealistic view of the American Indian. The Dartmouth Indians have become, for the past as well as the present, the Dartmouth Green, the Green Machine, and, in their own considered estimation, undoubtedly supreme among the Ivies.

For the first 11 years, Dartmouth teams were led by captains. It wasn't until 1893, when Wallace Moyle, an ex-Yale end, came to Hanover, that Dartmouth had its first coach and its first championship. Moyle's teams won 9 of 16 games in his two seasons which included a 34-0 dump of Amherst for the New

England Championship. The years between 1895 and 1901 were largely uneventful. Then, Walter McCornack '97 returned to Hanover in 1901 and changed all that. McCornack, who had been experimenting with coaching techniques at Exeter, brought some of his players with him. He set up one of the toughest schedules Dartmouth had played to date and the Green obliged him with a 9-1 season, shutting out New Hampshire State, Trinity, Boston College, Tufts, Vermont and Brown. The only defeat came from Harvard, 27-12. The 1902 team ranked among the nation's top 10 with a 6-2-1 record.

Fred Folsom '93 took over for McCornack in 1903. In his first season, Dartmouth shut out its first five opponents. The Green was considered for the National Championship until Princeton shut them out in their sixth game. That less-than-perfect record, 9-1-0, included one of their most memorable games. On 14 November 1903, the Green journeyed to Cambridge to inaugurate Harvard's new stadium. Before a crowd of 20,000, the Green recovered a fumble on the second play of the game and drove in for the touchdown. Harvard never recovered. In Hanover the 11-0 victory was called 'the greatest feat in Dartmouth's athletic history.'

In the next two years, 1904 and 1905, Dartmouth was defeated only once, in 1905 by Colgate (16-10) whose spirited play and mischievous tricks bewildered the Green. The only blemish on the 1904 season was a frustrating scoreless tie with Harvard. One of the Green's first football heroes came out of this era: Ralph Glaze '06. Glaze, chosen by Walter Camp as the greatest end of the 1905 season, was the smallest man on the team. He stood 5-feet 8-inches and weighed only 153 pounds, yet he

Above: *The 1881 team played its first intercollegiate game against Amherst at home in Hanover.*

Page 78: *The Big Green faces the field before a game on a crisp New England autumn afternoon.*

Page 79: *The Dartmouth Green versus the Brown Bruins on 14 November 1987.*

Far left: *In Fred Folsom's first season as coach in 1903 the then-called Dartmouth Indians shut out its first five opponents.*

Left: *One of Dartmouth's first football heroes, Ralph Glaze '06 was designated the greatest end in 1905 by Walter Camp.*

Below: *In 1903 Harvard's new stadium was inaugurated with this touchdown by Dartmouth, which set back the Crimson in an 11-0 defeat.*

was wiry and muscular, a versatile football player and a tough tackler.

J C O'Connor continued to provide great football seasons at Dartmouth when he took over for Folsom in 1907. That year, Dartmouth allowed only 10 points to its opponents – all in a game at Amherst (15-10). The next year Harvard returned its shutout with one of its own, 6-0, and Dartmouth ended the season with an overall 6-1-1.

In 1911, Frank Cavanaugh came to campus. Cavanaugh is remembered for his great stories; his powers of oratory roused his elevens to victory after victory. As coach, Cav believed in courage and strength more than strategy and finesse; his teams gave up no more than two games a season. In his six seasons, Dartmouth scored nearly 1400 points, allowing only 250 against them. Three of those points came during an astonishing shutout at Princeton when the Tigers scored one of the weirdest field goals in history. Wallace DeWitt, faced with an onrushing Dartmouth team, had to hurry his kick. It flew low, bounced once, then twice, then jumped over the crossbar at the last moment. Called valid by the referee, the goal gave the Tigers its 3-0 win. A rules change the next year ensured that such a field goal would remain history.

In 1917, the 40-year-old Cavanaugh left

Hanover for the war in Europe saying, 'I've got to go. I can't stay away. In that thing over there are the boys I have coached. I've tried to teach them courage and sacrifice and loyalty to an ideal. But we're only playing at it in a thing that's but a game. Now, God give them strength, they're lining up there where there isn't any fooling. It's death or glory now. I've got to go with them.' Cav enlisted as a private, advanced to major and was seriously wounded in the last three weeks of fighting. When he returned stateside, it was to Boston College for more football. Cavanaugh was the first of Dartmouth's coaches elected to the National Football Hall of Fame.

With Cavanaugh gone, Dartmouth turned to Clarence Spears '17. An All-America guard in 1915, Spears, at 5-foot 7-inches and 241 pounds, earned the nickname 'Fats.' In 1918, Spears coached a team made up of participants in the Student's Army Training Corps for a 3-3 season. Spears stayed at Dartmouth through the 1920 season, winning 21 of 31 games. His last game saw the Green to their first West Coast victory, with a 27-7 defeat of Washington. Spears, the second of Dartmouth's coaches to be elected to the Football Hall of Fame, left Hanover for Minnesota in 1921. Among those he coached, tackle Edward Francis Healy '17 has a place in both the College and Pro Football Hall of Fame. Healy saw the Green through five winning games in 1917 before he was sidelined with injuries. Dartmouth lost its last three games without the powerful tackle. He was also one of the first Dartmouth students to enlist in World War I.

Jackson Cannell '19 took over where Spears left off. Cannell coached a total of seven seasons at Dartmouth, 1921 to 1922 and again from 1929 to 1933. In his first stint, Cannell saw Dartmouth through its 200th win in a southern raid on Georgia. The 7-0 shutout was the first major northern victory on southern soil since the Civil War. The only touchdown of the game came from a fifty-yard pass launched by the injured Jim Robertson '20 to waiting Ed Lynch '23. Other heroes of the game included Pudge Neidlinger '23, who added the extra point, and Charles Calder.

Between 1923 and 1928, Dartmouth was coached by businessman Jesse Hawley '09. Hawley is credited with bringing the team into the twentieth century by applying business principles to football – he was a strategist, and a charter of strengths and weaknesses. He chartered his eleven right through a National Championship in 1925 with the likes of Andrew 'Swede' Oberlander '26. Hawley's elevens gave up only one game from 1923

through the first three games of the 1926 season. The team which defeated Dartmouth was itself undefeated – the great Big Red eleven of Gilmour Dobie. Cornell took the opportunity of Dartmouth's dedication of Memorial Field in 1923 to perpetuate its winning streak, 32-7.

By his second season, Hawley, through his principle of building on his team's strengths, had developed the forward pass into an instrument of destruction. It was nowhere more deadly than when launched by Swede Oberlander to the rhythm 'ten thousand Swedes jumped out of the weeds at the Battle of Copenhagen.' In 1924, Dartmouth was undefeated; the only blemish on the season was a

14-14 tie against also-undefeated Yale. The Green shut out Norwich, McGill, Vermont, Harvard and Boston University, and they paid back Cornell, 27-14.

Dartmouth was swamped with accolades for its 1925 team. They were considered the first of the modern Dartmouth elevens in pioneering the forward pass. The Green shut out its first four opponents, and it allowed Harvard only 9 points to 32 for a third consecutive win over the Crimson. Then Brown was shut out, and the stage was set for Cornell. The Big Red, returning to Memorial Field, were not prepared for the aerial game which Hawley had planned. Four secret pass plays had been developed especially for the Cornell game. Oberlander completed pass after pass for 48 points, including one 50-yard touchdown run. Cornell continually elected to kick off its return, something teams would avoid doing in response to this new aerial game in the future. When the bloodbath was over, the Big Red were dead, 64-13. It was, in one former Yale player's words, 'the most perfect exhibition of forward passing and play deception that I think I have ever seen on any field.' Oberlander

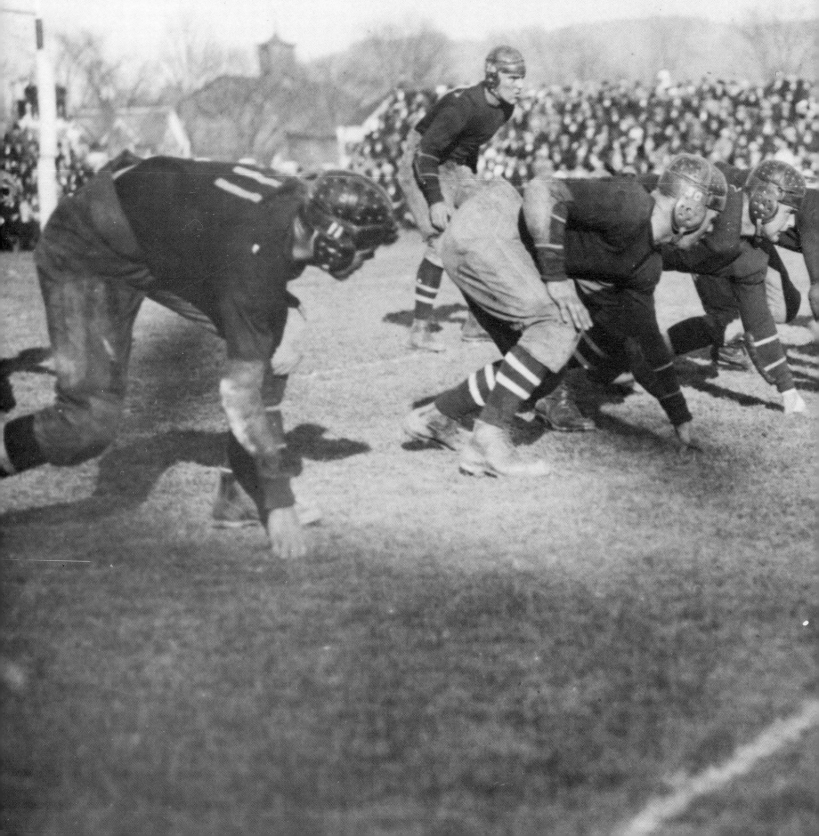

set a new Dartmouth record with his six touchdown passes, but Dartmouth wasn't quite finished yet.

The last game of 1925 was played against defending Big Ten champion University of Chicago and Coach Amos Alonzo Stagg. The game caught national headlines; Knute Rockne favored Dartmouth for its forward pass, others favored Chicago for its 'jump shift' offensive formation. More than 8000 alumni and students, including President Ernest M Hopkins, travelled to Chicago to watch Dartmouth avoid Chicago's defensive line with double-pass Statue of Liberty plays, hidden-ball pass plays, and end runs. Dartmouth gained 182 yards in the air for a final score of 33-7. Said Coach Stagg, 'our defensive play against your forward passes was dumb.'

Other stars of the undefeated elevens of those years were Heinie Sage, Oberlander's favorite receiver, and Myles Joseph Lane '28. In his three years as regular left halfback for Dartmouth, Lane scored 308 points. Both Oberlander and Lane are in the College Football Hall of Fame.

Hawley's winning streak ended abruptly at

Below: The first game played on Dartmouth's Memorial Field in 1923 pitted the undefeated Green against the undefeated Big Red. The latter prevailed, 32-7.

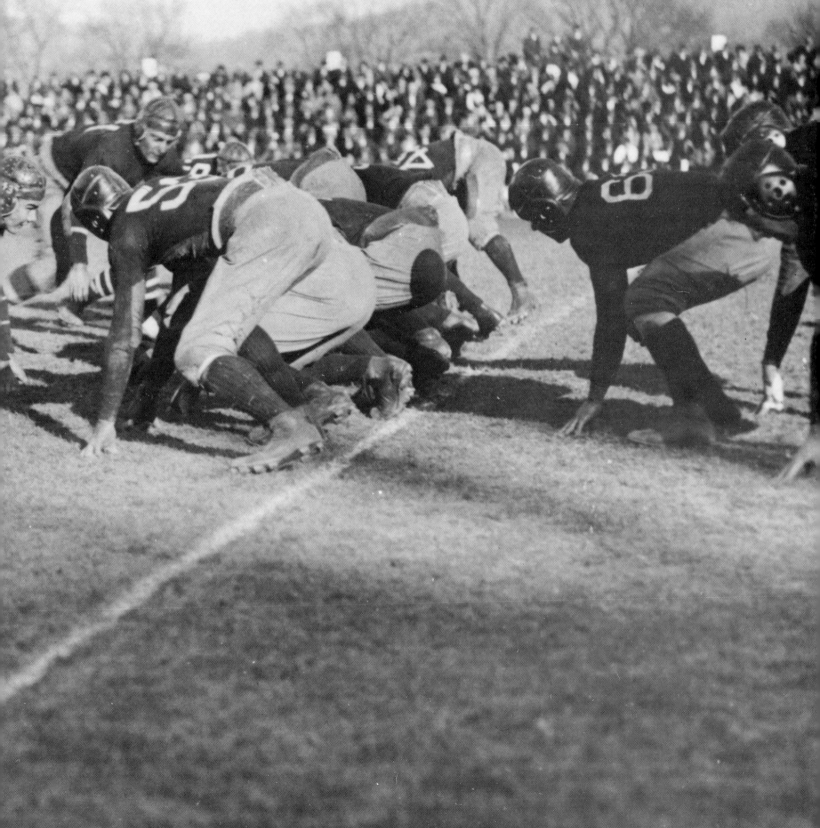

Left: *Football Hall of Famer Myles Lane scored a total of 308 points as Dartmouth's left halfback from 1925-1928.*

Above: *Al 'Special Delivery' Marsters, considered by many to be the greatest back in Dartmouth history, is shown here in cap and gown in 1930.*

Right: *QB Bill Morton was the Green's star from 1930-32, scoring 25 TDs in three seasons.*

22 games in 1926, when the Green played Yale. The Elis were the only Ivy team Dartmouth had played and never beaten – it was called the Yale jinx. (Dartmouth didn't play Yale in its 1925 season.) In 1928, Hawley's last season at Dartmouth, the team was troubled with injuries. It took defeats from Harvard, Yale, Brown and Northwestern. Hawley decided to go back to business full-time, lured by the Coolidge years of prosperity. He left behind a thoroughly modern team with a winning legacy that would last a long time.

When Cannell resumed his coaching duties in 1929, he came back to a team recovered from injuries and ready to fight. Again, Dartmouth took an undefeated record to Yale, this time with Alton 'Special Delivery' Marsters '30. Marsters has been called the greatest back in Dartmouth history. In the second half of the Yale game, Marsters moved Dartmouth to the Yale 30 from the Dartmouth 10 by completing two passes and receiving another. With a series of line plunges, Marsters set up the Green's first touchdown. A second touchdown run by Marsters put Dartmouth ahead, but Marsters had wrenched his back and was taken out. Yale went on to a 16-12 victory. Marsters was named to the All-America team in 1929, but his football career ended that season with his injury at Yale.

Cannell replaced his Special Delivery with William 'Air Mail' Morton '32, an untried sophomore. In his first game, against Brown, Morton won it almost single-handedly, 13-6. He scored 25 touchdowns in three seasons and was elected to the Football Hall of Fame. Dartmouth's 1930 overall was 7-1-1, with a scoreless tie against Yale and a defeat from powerful Stanford.

Cannell's most memorable game probably came in 1931. Again, Yale was the opponent and Dartmouth was behind, 26-10 at the half. Yale scored again to make it 33 but Dartmouth's Wild Bill McCall broke loose taking the kickoff 94 yards for a touchdown. The Green blocked a Yale kick and ran in for another touchdown. McCall made a one-handed grab to snatch a pass meant for Eli Albie Booth and raced 60 yards for a third touchdown. With Dartmouth trailing by three, Air Mail Morton, at a third down with 14 yards to go, dropped back to the 24-yard line and, with McCall holding the ball, kicked for 34 yards and a field goal to make it 33-33. The Yale jinx was seeing better days, but would not be broken in Cannell's term. His last two seasons, 1932 and 1933, were 4-4-0 and 4-4-1. After the 1933 season, he was replaced by Earl Henry Blaik.

Blaik, the result of a major search for a new head coach, was the first non-grad to be hired by the school. He established an atmosphere of spartan discipline, sacrifice and tough practices. The Dartmouth elevens learned to submerge the individual for the benefit of the whole, and, on the whole, it paid off. Blaik had good material to work with, too, with Robert 'Wildfire' MacLeod '39, Gregory 'Gus' Zitrides '39, as well as the undefeated elevens of the 1937 season.

In Blaik's first season at Dartmouth, the Green shut out their first five opponents. They lost only to Yale, Cornell and Princeton. His second season brought about the victory for which Dartmouth had waited 52 years: Dartmouth beat Yale, 14-6. The game began with Dartmouth's Jack Kenny '36 almost getting his helmet blown off when he stuck his head in a Yale huddle and said, 'Let's have some fun today, boys.' Dartmouth's Pop Nairne '36 scored early for the first touchdown. The 7-0 lead held until the second half when Yale intercepted a Dartmouth punt, evaded John Handrahan's tackle lunge and scored. Yale missed the conversion. It was late in the fourth quarter. A desperate Eli quarterback passed into the receptive arms of Dartmouth linebacker Carl 'Mutt' Ray '37 who obliged his team by running it in for the final touchdown. Jubilant Dartmouth fans ran onto the field and tore down the goal posts with two minutes left on the clock.

Princeton and a tough Columbia team were the only ones to down the Green in 1935. In New Jersey, it was the 'Battle of the Blizzard,' a game made famous by Dartmouth's mysterious twelfth man. Princeton was ahead 20-6 in the fourth quarter and ready on the Dart-

Above: Coach Earl Henry 'Red' Blaik incorporated spartan discipline into his Dartmouth troops. Highlights of the Blaik years (1934-40) included a long-awaited victory over Yale and a 22-game winning streak.

Below: *A tombstone erected on the Dartmouth campus memorializes the 1935 game in which the Green finally broke the Yale jinx with a score of 14-6.*

Bottom: *Bob Blackman renewed Dartmouth's fortunes from 1955-71 with seven Ivy championships, two Lambert Trophies and an impressive 104-37-3 record.*

mouth two when, from the stands, a man charged into the line yelling, 'Kill them Princeton bastards!' The mystery man, never identified, dodged tacklers and prevented a Princeton score. Princeton prevailed in the end, 26-6.

The following three seasons were great ones for Blaik and Dartmouth. In 1936, working off a jinx of their own, Holy Cross handed Dartmouth its only defeat of the season, 7-0. It was the first time the school had beaten the Green since the two started playing in 1903. After that, the Green embarked on a 22-game winning streak that didn't end until the Green met the Big Red in the next-to-last game of the

1938 season. Blaik had built his team around the strengths of one halfback: Robert MacLeod '39. MacLeod impressed everyone with his style, grace and skill.

At the beginning of 1937, Blaik thought he was riding a 'dark, dark horse,' but the Green pulled it off, scoring 248 points while allowing only 33. Harvard was halted in a driving rainstorm and held to only two points to Dartmouth's 20. 'Bombshell Bill' Hutchinson emerged as a hero of the game for his ability to wiggle through lines and run like hell, very much like Jesse Owens with whom he was compared. The MacLeod and Hutchinson

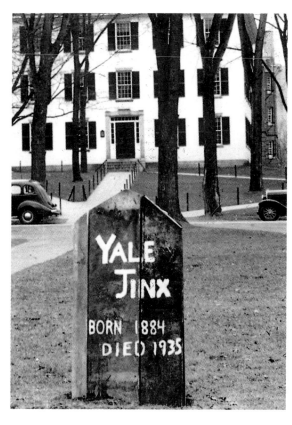

Below: *Blaik's backfield force in 1938 (l-r): Bob MacLeod, who was elected to 14 All-America teams and the Football Hall of Fame, Sanford Courtier, Colby Howe, and 'Bombshell Bill' Hutchinson.*

attack was held to a tie by both Yale and Cornell, leaving the Green with a 7-0-2 overall at the end of 1937 and an invitation to the Rose Bowl. President Hopkins, even though he supported football, turned the invitation down because 'football was incidental to the purpose for which the player was in college.'

The elevens continued undefeated through the first seven games of 1938 until they met Cornell at Ithaca. The Green could not get past their tormentors until they resorted to two consecutive Statue of Liberty plays for one touchdown, 14-7. At Stanford, and despite valiant defensive work by MacLeod, the Green

lost, 23-13. For his eight touchdowns in 1938 and his tough defensive work, MacLeod was elected to 14 All-America teams and later to the National Football Hall of Fame.

Blaik stayed on for two more seasons, 5-3-1 and 5-4-0. It was a hard decision for him, but after the 1940 season he elected to become Army's head football coach. His last season was made memorable by the famous fifth-down game against Cornell. The struggle, carried out in the mud and snow of Memorial Field, pitted the Big Red 18-game winning streak against a Green 3-4 season. Through the first three quarters, the game was scoreless. Then, Dartmouth's Bob Krieger kicked a 27-yard field goal to make it 3-0. In the last minute of play, with Cornell on the Dartmouth two, the Big Red were hit with a penalty for delaying play. In the next play, a Big Red pass was batted down – but was it a fourth down pass, or a third down pass? Referee Red Friesell awarded Cornell another play, and Cornell made its touchdown. Although the press were certain the game had been won on a fifth down, the truth did not come out until the films were reviewed. On Monday, Cornell telegraphed Dartmouth conceding the error and their defeat.

DeOrmond 'Tuss' McLaughry, who replaced Blaik, came to Dartmouth from Brown and the infamous 1926 Brown team. In the first two years of World War II, he had 4-5 overalls before leaving the school to help with the war effort. Only in 1948 and 1949 did McLaughry have winning seasons. In 1948, Dartmouth defeated all but Pennsylvania and Cornell. In 1949, Dartmouth lost to the Tigers, 19-13, and was shut out by Penn, 21-0. One of McLaughry's most memorable games was played in New Jersey on 13 November 1950, during Hurricane Flora. Flora's winds blew out plate glass windows, uprooted trees on campus and downed telephone and telegraph lines at Palmer Stadium. Still, the game went on. There was so much water on the field that the referees had to hold the ball for the snap so it would not float away. Despite an early lead on a 23-yard run by Bob Tyler '51, Princeton came back for two, and the 13-7 halftime score held to the muddy end.

After five straight losing seasons, Dartmouth decided against renewing McLaughry's contract. The future Hall of Famer was replaced by Bob Blackman who, for the next 16 years, would coach the Green through its most successful seasons ever. In Blackman's tenure, Dartmouth had only two losing seasons, was Ivy League champ seven times and twice Lambert Trophy winners. Blackman had

Right: *In this November 1949 game Dartmouth decisively leaped over Columbia, 35-14.*

Below: *In the memorable 13 November 1950 game both Dartmouth and Princeton defied an additional opponent: Hurricane Flora. As Flora's torrents uprooted trees and flooded the field, Princeton predominated over the Green, 13-7.*

a history of turning things around – from his own bout with polio in college, to the teams at Pasadena City College and the University of Denver, both of which he turned into champions. Blackman adapted to the strictly volunteer football program at Dartmouth by challenging his players not only with demanding practices but also with the variations on plays he was forever thinking up. The Green had hundreds of tricks to pull out of their helmets and keep the game going in their favor. Perhaps the most startling was the 'human steps' formation which required foam rubber shoes and was used to launch the Green over the Princeton line. Blackman also invented the V-formation, tackle-eligible pass plays, deceptive kick returns, and laterals going the width of the field.

It took Blackman exactly one season to get his team turned around. In 1955, Dartmouth mustered wins over only Harvard, Columbia and Cornell. The Ivy League had its first official season in 1956, and the Green squeaked through, beating Brown, Columbia, Cornell and Princeton for a 5-3-1 overall. In 1957, the Green landed a 5-1-1 record which included shutouts of Brown, Harvard and Columbia. The next year, the Green moved from second place to first in the League when they beat everyone but Harvard. The 1958 season pales, though, in comparison to 1962.

Dartmouth's last unbeaten and untied season had been in 1925, and 37 years later the Green had finally done it again. The 1962 season was brought off in part on the abilities of William Haven King '63, whom Blackman called 'my right arm.' King, team captain and quarterback, was the eleven's best runner, passer and kicker, in Blackman's estimation. His school record for total offense in a single game is still unbeaten in Hanover: 348 yards against Columbia in 1962. Halfback Tom Spangenberg set the record in 1962 for the longest interception pass returned when he snitched a pass at the Dartmouth four and returned it all the way for a 10-0 win over Holy Cross. The Green shut out Brown for a fourth year, and downed Massachusetts and Penn. King scored two of the touchdowns against Harvard, 24-6, and set up the field goal which broke a scoreless game at Yale, 9-0. In Hanover, King completed 14 of 16 passes and threw for four touchdowns to embarrass Columbia, 42-0. After their 28-21 squeaker over Cornell, the Green were number two in Lambert balloting and were set to face Princeton. Dartmouth had a title on the line, but Princeton had a grudge. The year before, Dartmouth had foiled Princeton's attempt at a

three-way championship with Columbia and Harvard. With touchdowns by Spangenberg and King, plus a field goal by Bill Wellstead, Dartmouth put Princeton away, 38-27, and took possession of its second Ivy title.

In 1963 Dartmouth had a 15-game winning streak, the longest in the country, going into the Harvard game at Cambridge. Harvard was enjoying a winning season, and despite a 74-yard scoring drive, Dartmouth was defeated 17-13 and had to share the Ivy title with Princeton. The next year, Dartmouth retaliated by holding Harvard scoreless, 48-0. But the Green was defeated by Princeton, Yale and Cornell for a number four position in the League in 1964.

In 1965, the Green were back for another championship season: untied, undefeated and, for the first time, Lambert Trophy winners. To do it, Dartmouth would have to confront the 17-game winning streak of Princeton. Dartmouth held New Hampshire and Holy Cross to one touchdown each and took Penn, 21-19. Harvard, Columbia and Cornell were powerless to score against the Green, and Yale fell by three, 20-17. The big game came last when

Above: Referee Red Friesell, who goofed during the 1940 Dartmouth-Cornell game in granting the Big Red a fifth down which enabled them to win. After reviewing the game on film, Cornell conceded defeat to Dartmouth at the fourth-down score of 3-0.

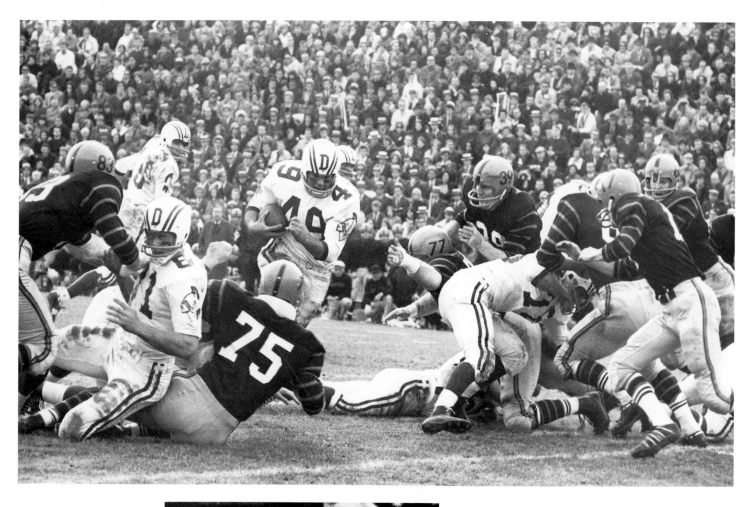

Above: *In this 1965 confrontation the Green completed an untied, undefeated season by ending Princeton's 17-game winning streak. The 28-14 score brought Dartmouth the Ivy championship and its first Lambert Trophy.*

Right: *The untied, undefeated 1962 season was spearheaded by captain and QB William Haven King, who still holds the school record for total offense in a single game (348 yards against Columbia in 1962.)*

Dartmouth had to put away the Tigers. Princeton opened with a 69-yard scoring drive which Dartmouth didn't tie until the second quarter on an 86-yard drive by Mickey Beard '67. Beard did it again before the quarter was over to put Dartmouth ahead for the rest of the game. The Green astonished Princeton's Charlie Gogolak with Blackman's human steps play. Sam Hawken, wearing foam rubber shoes, leapt off the backs of crouching linesmen as Gogolak attempted his field goal. Hawkins, though, landed over the Princeton line before the ball was called into play and was offsides; still, the startled Gogolak missed the goal. In the end, with two more touchdowns, Dartmouth had it, 28-14.

Blackman's elevens did not stop there. In 1966 and 1969, the team was again co-champ in the Ivies. In 1966 the title was shared with Harvard and Princeton, and in 1969 with Yale and Princeton. In 1970, Dartmouth had it all to themselves.

The 1970 team gave up only 42 points the whole season, better than any college in the nation. The 1970 Green Machine was made up of strong performers like quarterback Jim Chasey, who passed for more than 1000 yards and six touchdowns; main running backs John Short and Brendan O'Neill '72, who combined for more than 1200 yards on the ground; and Murray Bowden '71, the calf roper from Texas

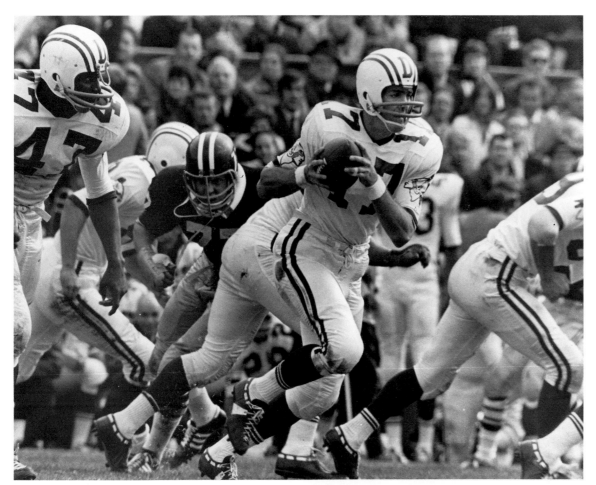

Left: *Carrying the ball is the Green's QB Jim Chasey, who in 1970 passed for more than 1000 yards and six touchdowns.*

Below: *Smiling with Dartmouth's second Lambert Trophy before him is Bob Blackman in 1970. To his right stands Murray Bowden '71 who had five interceptions to his credit.*

who brought down the likes of Cornell's Ed Marinaro and had five interceptions. The 1970 Green shut out six teams, five of them Ivies: Princeton, Yale, Columbia, Cornell and Penn. Dartmouth ended the season ranked fourteenth nationally and took its second Lambert Trophy.

At the Harvard game that year, sportswriters later quipped that the Cantabs 'came up Short' in their 37-14 loss; Dartmouth's John Short carried 25 times for 106 yards and two touchdowns, and passed for another. When Dartmouth rolled into New Haven, it was a battle of the champions, but Dartmouth, with 480 yards of total offense, never gave the Elis a chance: 10-0. Columbia gave Dartmouth the greatest Ivy victory margin ever: 55-0. At Cornell, Bowden, his shoulder in a special harness to keep the joint intact, kept Marinaro and Cornell scoreless: 24-0. The winningest season ever ended with a shutout of Penn, with Chasey and Short scoring all the touchdowns.

The season's end did hold some sadness for Dartmouth. Blackman, who had rolled up an astonishing 104-37-3 record in 16 years at Hanover, wanted another challenge. He left in 1971 for the Fighting Illini of the University of Illinois, and was replaced by the man who held Dartmouth's rushing record until 1973, Jake Crouthamel '60.

Crouthamel's first three years at Dartmouth

were championship years. In 1971, Dartmouth shared the crown with Cornell. The only team to beat Dartmouth was Columbia, 31-29, but at the Harvard game it was close. The Crimson had Dartmouth tied, 13-13, up to the last two seconds of play. With 18 seconds on the clock, safety Wesley Pugh '72 intercepted a Harvard fourth-down pass and took it to the Harvard 38. In the last six seconds, quarterback Bill Pollock '72 threw to halfback Doug Lind '74 on the Harvard 29 and Ted Perry '74 lined up for the snap. Harvard had blocked two of Perry's field goal attempts, but this time he connected and sent Dartmouth to victory, 16-13.

The 1972 championship season was a cliffhanger. Dartmouth, which tied Harvard and was beaten by Yale, had to fight for its last two games, against Cornell and Penn. Three times in the second half at Ithaca the Green found itself defending its ten-yard line against a Big Red attack. In the last two minutes of the game, Rick Klupchak whizzed through a hole at the Dartmouth 28 and ended up in the Cornell end zone: 31-22. The next Saturday, the Quakers held Dartmouth tied 17-all until the last two minutes of the fourth quarter, when the Green scored two touchdowns in two minutes. The first came on a pass from Steve Stetson '73 to Chuck Thomas '73, and the second on a run by Steve Webster '73. Meanwhile, Harvard downed Yale to give the Green its fourth straight championship.

Dartmouth did it again in 1973, coming away from three losses early to six straight wins for a 6-1 Ivy overall. Only Pennsylvania defeated the Green, 22-16, in a season that saw Klupchak break his own coach's record. It happened at Princeton, when Klupchak scored three touchdowns and surpassed Crouthamel's rushing record by 25 yards.

In 1974, Dartmouth had its first losing season since 1968 and tied for fifth, with Princeton, in the league. In 1975 the Green rebounded with assistance from such great players as Reginald Williams '76, who was named All-America in recognition of his talents as a linebacker. At Dartmouth, Williams led the school in both tackles and assists to bring down 370 opponents. Dartmouth moved up to fourth place in 1975. The next year the Green shared third ranking in the league with Harvard. In 1977, only Harvard, Brown and Penn beat the Green. That year, Crouthamel decided he had had enough of coaching and left the game. He was replaced by Dartmouth's first choice for coach to replace Blackman back in 1971: Joe Yukica, coach at Boston College.

In Yukica's nine years at Dartmouth, he

Opposite top: *Jake Crouthamel '60, whose first years of coaching saw the Green Machine achieve another three championships. The end of his term saw Dartmouth sink uncharacteristically below third in the Ivies.*

Above: *The Green fight to stave off the Big Red defense in 1972. In the last two minutes Rick Klupchak scrambled through a chink in the Cornell defense at the Dartmouth 28 to grab a TD and the fourth consecutive championship.*

Left: *With only three seconds left in the 1971 showdown, with Harvard and Dartmouth tied 13-13, the Green's Ted Perry kicked a 46-yard field goal to defeat the Crimson 16-13.*

Right: *Dartmouth QB Chris Rorke (7) intent on spotting a receiver in a 1987 game.*

Middle right: *Dartmouth coach Buddy Teevens '79 explaining a play to Craig Morton.*

Bottom right: *During coach Joe Yukica's tenure (1978-86), Dartmouth's losing seasons were sweetened by three championships: the title in 1978, a shared title with Yale in 1981, and a triple tie with Penn and Harvard in 1982.*

Below: *Sophomore LB Christopher Balish (98) rubbing up against the Yale defensive line in 1985.*

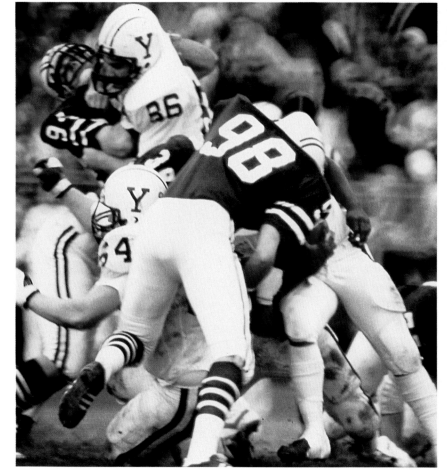

Above: *The Green Machine's Dave Shula '81, known for his gymnastic exploits, dodges a determined New Hampshire tackle in 1980.*

brought back championship seasons. He told his 1978 team, 'this will not be a rebuilding year at Dartmouth. Our goal will be the Ivy League title, nothing less.' The 1978 eleven had lost 27 lettermen and five All-Ivy players to the world of alumni, but they didn't let that stop them. With such players as quarterback Eugene 'Buddy' Teevens '79 to rewrite the school's record books, and aerial artists like David Shula '81 and Jeff Kemp '81, the Green took the championship on one loss to Harvard and a 6-3 overall season. The next two seasons were losers for the Green, with 4-4-1 and 4-6-0 overall records. Dartmouth came back again, though, in 1981, to share the title with Yale, the only Ivy team to beat them. In 1982, on a 5-5 overall, Dartmouth again notched a hold at the top in a three-way tie with Penn and Harvard.

The remaining four years of Yukica's tenure were poor seasons at Dartmouth. In 1983, the Green were 4-5-1 overall, 4-2-1 Ivy and shared third place with Brown. Through 1986, though, the Green won only two games a season. In 1987, Dartmouth brought in Buddy Teevens '79 from the University of Maine to replace Yukica. Teevens was responsible for bringing back winning seasons in Orono. In 1987, though, the Green beat only Columbia in Ivy action. Dartmouth has 13 championships under its collective belt, however, and the winningest record in the league. Chances are the turnaround is not long in coming.

HARVARD UNIVERSITY

Founded: 1636
Location: Cambridge, Massachusetts
Undergraduate Enrollment: 6568
Color: Crimson
Nickname: Crimson

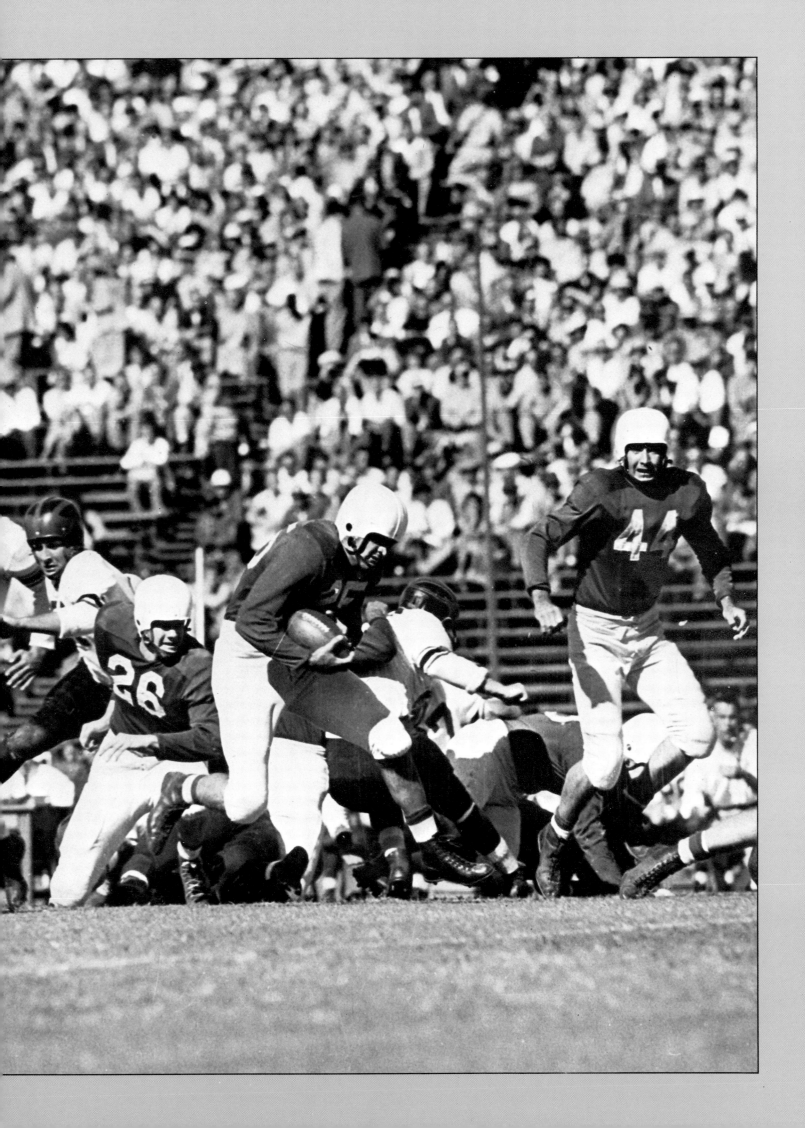

Page 98: *QB Tom Yohe in 1987.*

Page 99: *The Harvard Crimson meet the Stanford Indians in the 1949 season opener.*

Above: *The first Crimson team, which was formed in 1874: (l-r, standing): Whiting, Randall, Leeds, Sanger and Lombard; (l-r, seated) Morse, Goodrich, team captain Grant, Tyler and Lyman.*

Top right: *Such was the popularity of what was to become Ivy League football that political cartoonist Thomas Nast commented on a Princeton victory over powerful Harvard with this drawing, captioned 'One Good Kick Deserves Another. O'er Harvard's sands the far reflections steal,/ Where mighty Princeton stamped her iron–toe.'*

In 1974, Harvard University's football family decided to do it up Crimson and celebrate 100 years of intercollegiate football. The Harvards had first taken the field in 1874 against Montreal's McGill University, and the centennial bore a certain elitist if bemused flavor when the celebration logo emerged as 'Harvard Football: The "Real" Centennial.'

Having a clear claim to the title as the nation's oldest college, Harvard was on somewhat shakier ground with its claim to have played the first 'real' football game in 1874. The argument as to who played by which rules in those early days has never been settled. And while it was unlikely to be settled by the Harvard centennial boast, the year was at least successful enough on the field for Harvard to share a piece of the 1974 Ivy League title.

Success in football has been Harvard's more often than not in the 1013 games the Crimson have played through the 1987 season. Thousands of Harvard men have played for 17 head coaches in 113 seasons since it all began against McGill in 1874. But the story of Harvard football goes far beyond such statistics. As with all colleges, it is a story of personalities and great moments, of individuals and teams. And in Harvard's particular case, of days to remember at 'the Stadium.'

Nearly 30 years of Harvard football teams established a successful tradition before the famous Harvard Stadium doors opened in 1903. The pre-Stadium teams compiled a record of 214-36-9 through 1902 and, in the very first decade of this period, a familiar and infuriating pattern emerged. Harvard lost just 17 games in the first 10 years of play, but a

dozen of those losses came at the hands of arch-rivals Princeton and Yale. Even today, an otherwise successful season is considered by Harvard alumni to be considerably less so if Princeton and particularly Yale aren't among the victims.

If those two opponents weren't enough, early Harvard football had another nemesis: the faculty. In 1884, the degree of rough play on the field was such that Harvard's Committee on the Regulation of Athletic Sports recommended to the faculty that football be dropped at Harvard. Said the Committee, 'The nature of the game puts a premium on unfair play, inasmuch as such play is easy, is profitable if it succeeds, is unlikely to be detected by the referee, and if detected is very slightly punished.'

The result of such an indictment was that Harvard dropped football for the 1885 season. The game returned in 1886, with Harvard's first systematic use of coaches. With the exception of 1881, when Lucius Littauer coached the Crimson, Harvard captains had assumed coaching duties. In 1886, Captain William Brooks '87 appointed Frank Mason '84 as coach, and in 1890 the first semblance of a coaching staff emerged when A J Cumnock '91 and George Stewart '84 both led the squad. Two must have been better than one as Harvard went 11-0 that year, outscored its opponents by 550-12 and beat Yale for the first time in 12 tries.

In the years prior to 1903, nearly 40 Crimson gridders received some form of All-American recognition. Among the most notable were Charley Brewer '96, the running back who carried the ball in coach Lorin Deland's 'flying wedge,' and Marshall 'Ma' Newell '94, a Walter Camp All-American four times. Four others who gained fame in this era were Ben Dibblee '99, Percy Haughton '99, Charley Daly '01 and Bill Reid '01. All gained All-America status as players and all went on

Above: *A drawing of the 1875 Crimson football team.*

Left: *A chromoprint of a scrimmage between Harvard and the University of Pennsylvania in 1890.*

Right: *This 1898 illustration shows Harvard's Ben Dibblee going around Yale's end for 35 yards. The Game became an institution almost at the inception of football at Harvard.*

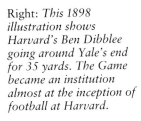

to coach at Harvard. These six players, along with David Campbell '02, are among 17 Harvard alumni enshrined in the National Football Hall of Fame.

The Harvard teams of 1901 and 1902 were coached by Bill Reid '01 and John Farley '99 respectively, and they won 23 straight games until they were defeated by Yale, 23-0, in the final game of the 1902 season. The 1902 campaign was also memorable because of a fire that destroyed a section of wooden bleachers at Soldiers Field. Harvard football had been played at Jarvis Field and Holmes Field before moving to the Soldiers Field area, but none of the sites had offered the permanence that was to come in 1903 with Harvard Stadium.

President Charles W Eliot, a former Crimson oarsman, recognized the need for a suitable structure to house Harvard football. Work began on the Stadium in June 1903 with hopes of being ready for the following season. Boston's Aberthaw Construction Company undertook the job that would eventually cost the University around $320,000. (By contrast, the Stadium's third press box, built in 1981 and used no more than a handful of days each year, cost $375,000.)

Harvard played its final non-Stadium home game on 31 October 1903, the day that coach Glenn 'Pop' Warner and the Carlisle Indians came to town with a trick-or-treat play. While forming a wedge on the second-half kickoff, the visiting Indians prepared to block for an apparent ball carrier named Johnson. What the Crimson defenders didn't see was that a would-be blocker named Dillon had tucked the ball under his shirt, and he ran virtually untouched the length of the field for a touchdown. Harvard had the treat, however, as the Crimson won the game, 12-11.

Two weeks later, when Harvard Stadium opened on 14 November, the home team was not as fortunate. Another group of Indians, from Hanover, New Hampshire, ruined Harvard's celebration. Dartmouth, 0-18 against Harvard up to that point, defeated the Crimson, 11-0. Nevertheless, Crimson football teams would win more than 70 percent of their home games during the next 80 years.

In January 1906, college football representatives met in New York at the request of President Theodore Roosevelt to discuss the increasing violence in college football. President Roosevelt, a Harvard man himself, had

Above: *The first touchdown at the new Harvard Stadium was scored by Dartmouth on 14 November 1903. The Crimson went down 11-0.*

Opposite top: *Coach Percy Haughton (center) poses with trainer Donovan and team captain Mahan for a preseason picture in 1915. One of the greatest football coaches ever, in his nine seasons as head coach at Harvard (1908-16), Haughton compiled a 71-7-5 record.*

Opposite bottom: *Seven of Harvard's greatest stars of the Haughton era: (l-r) Stan Pennock, All-America guard; Fred Bradlee, All-America halfback; Mal Logan, quarterback; Charlie Brickley, All-America halfback; Tack Hardwick, All-America end; Wally Trumbull, All-America tackle; and Jeff Coolidge, end.*

gone on record as saying, 'Brutality and foul play should receive the same summary punishment given to a man who cheats at cards.' The college administrators, led by Yale's Walter Camp and Harvard's Bill Reid, considered a number of measures that might open up the game and lessen brutality. One suggestion was to widen the field, an idea effectively squashed due to restraints the Stadium put on Harvard's playing field. And so the gentlemen introduced the forward pass to football.

Meanwhile, on the field, Harvard continued to be successful against just about everyone but Yale. From 1904 to 1911, Harvard lost just 11 times, but the eight meetings with Yale produced just one win. That came in 1908, the first year for Coach Percy Haughton. When Captain 'Hooks' Burr called on Haughton to lead Harvard, a new tradition emerged. Before Haughton, coaches stayed for only one or two seasons. Haughton coached for nine seasons and compiled a record of 71-7-5, arguably the best in Harvard history.

Some of Harvard's greatest played in the Haughton era, most notably running backs Eddie Mahan, Percy Wendell and Eddie Casey, and dropkick specialist Charlie Brickley. Said Notre Dame coach Jesse Harper of Haughton, 'Here was a great coach, not merely a good one . . . He was colder than an iceberg, harder than granite. But he was brilliant – a natural leader.

He was to football what General Patton was to our armies.'

Despite Haughton's brilliance, perhaps Harvard football's greatest accomplishment came after World War I had effectively ended the Haughton era. In 1919, Bob Fisher '12 succeeded Haughton as head coach. A former Crimson guard, Fisher coached for seven years, but enjoyed his greatest success in his first season, which took Harvard to Pasadena and the Rose Bowl. Behind the brilliant running of Eddie Casey, Harvard compiled an 8-0-1 mark en route to a stunning 7-6 win over Oregon on New Year's Day, 1920. The lone Harvard touchdown was scored by Fred Church, and the winning point came from the toe of Arnold Horween, Fisher's successor as head coach.

Horween coached from 1926 through 1930. His early teams featured the likes of Art French, Joe Crosby and Dave Guarnaccia. But it was the inspired play of Ben Ticknor and, most notably, Barry Wood from his final teams that left the greatest impression on Harvard football. W Barry Wood '32 might just have been Harvard's greatest athlete. He won ten varsity letters – three each in football, hockey, and baseball, and his final 'H' as a tennis player on the joint Harvard-Yale team that competed against Oxford-Cambridge for the Prentice Cup. He was a first team All-American in 1931 and graduated *summa cum laude* before moving on to Johns Hopkins Medical School, where he would one day return as a research specialist.

Barry Wood's athletic career at Harvard included some of the greatest moments in Harvard athletic history. A great era began in 1929 when the sophomore quarterback came off the bench against Army to hit Victor Harding with a 40-yard touchdown pass that, along with Wood's extra-point kick, knotted the Cadets at 20-20. Two years later, he crafted one of the school's most celebrated victories when he led two touchdown drives to put Harvard up 14-13 over Army and then made a game-saving tackle on defense to preserve the win.

It was also in this era that Wood staged a series of heroic battles with his Yale counterpart, Albie Booth. Beginning in their freshman season, Wood and Booth enjoyed center stage in both football and baseball battles. In their

Below: QB Barry Wood (in top left of photo) takes a lateral pass from teammate Devens in 1931. A superb all-around athlete, Wood's strong play was pivotal to the Crimson squads of 1929-31. His showdowns with Yale's Albie Booth made The Game particularly exciting during that era.

freshman game, it was Wood's point-after that decided a 7-6 affair. In the first of three varsity games, Wood's toe again provided the margin of victory as Harvard won, 10-6. In their junior year, Wood clearly outshone Booth as the Harvardian threw two touchdown passes to Art Huguley in a 13-0 victory. But Booth was to have his moment in the final football meeting of the two.

It was 1931 and Harvard entered the Yale game with a 7-0 record and hopes of its first perfect season since 1913. Late in the fourth quarter, the two teams were locked in a 0-0 stalemate. With Harvard denied by the stubborn Yale defense, Wood went back to punt, but Yale's Jack Wilbur broke through the line for the block. Yale took over and began to move the ball behind Booth. With time ticking away and three years of frustration very much in mind, Booth calmly kicked the winning field goal for a 3-0 Yale triumph.

The years between Barry Wood and World War II brought the first non-Harvard man to the position of head coach. Dick Harlow's 11-year career started and ended with difficulty. In his third season, after two losing cam-

paigns, Harlow's defense began to shine. With the likes of two-way players Alex Kevorkian and Ken Booth, Harvard allowed only 19 points all season against a tough schedule that

Top: *Coach Arnold Horween (right) with Knute Rockne in 1929. Captain of the 1920 Crimson team, Horween went on to coach at his alma mater for five seasons (1926-30).*

Above: *Dick Harlow coached the Crimson for 11 seasons, 1935-42 and 1945-47.*

Left: *Coach Bob Fisher (center) with Captain Marion Cheek (left) and the previous season's captain, Mal Greenough, in 1925.*

Top: *John F Kennedy (second row from top, second from right) played on Harvard's junior varsity team in 1937. A back injury suffered that year ended his football career.*

Above: *Tackle Chester Pierce '48.*

included Army, Navy, Princeton and Yale. Said noted football historian Tim Cohane, 'Harvard's football teams of the 1930s were pioneers of stunting in their defensive line play. By looping or slanting just before or at the snap of the ball, they were never where they were supposed to be when opponents tried to block them.'

In addition to skilled defense, Harlow had two exceptional running backs in Vernon Struck, whose records still stand, and Torbert Macdonald, John F Kennedy's roommate and later a U S Congressman. Struck's 233 yards against Princeton remains a record today and helped end Harvard's three-game losing streak to the Tigers. Macdonald wasn't the only future politician to shine for Harlow. Perhaps the best of all Harlow's players was Endicott 'Chub' Peabody '42, a tough, physical guard who was a first team All-American in 1941 and later the governor of Massachusetts.

The story is told of the 1941 Navy game in which the 1-2 Crimson met the 4-0 Midshipmen. Navy was coached by Swede Nelson and led by All-American back Bill Busik. A bone-jarring Peabody tackle after a second-quarter punt caused Busik to fumble and knocked him out of the game. The contest ended in a 0-0 tie and Harvard, and Peabody, went on to win the final four games of the talented guard's All-American season.

When World War II broke out, Harlow temporarily gave up the Harvard football reins to Henry Lamar and went off to war. When he returned, he coached three more seasons but was never the same man, affected by his wartime experience. The years immediately following the war were difficult for everyone involved, although the records of the 1945 and 1946 teams weren't bad – 5-3 and 7-2. Captain Cleo O'Donnell led the latter squad, which included fullback Vince Moravec, halfback Chip Gannon, end Wally Flynn and place-kicker Emil Drvaric.

The 1947 season featured an ugly incident involving a trip to Virginia, a school whose athletic administrators had suggested to Harvard athletic director Bill Bingham that per-

haps Harvard leave one player home. That player was tackle Chester Pierce whose appearance at Virginia would make him the first black player to play in an intersectional game below the Mason-Dixon line. Bingham's response was immediate and unmistakable. Either Pierce makes the trip or Harvard doesn't. The game went on, and unfortunately Harvard was beaten badly, 47-0.

Following Harlow's departure in 1948, Harvard football began a rather quick descent into mediocrity. Two coaches would struggle and a third would be needed to get Harvard back on top. In all, the next eleven seasons produced just three winning records and an overall mark of 36-53-3. The bottom fell out in 1949 and 1950 when the Crimson staggered through back-to-back seasons of 1-8 and 1-7.

Arthur Valpey, a former player and assistant coach at Michigan, followed Harlow to Cambridge but lasted only two years. After a 4-4 season in 1948, Valpey took his team to Stanford for the season opener in 1949, Harvard's first West Coast trip since winning the 1920

Above: *Harvard hits a stone wall trying to carry the ball through the Princeton line, 1935.*

Left: *Guard Endicott 'Chub' Peabody was All-America in 1941.*

Above: *Lloyd Jordan coached the Crimson for seven seasons (1950-56), with mixed results.*

Opposite, main picture: *Cantab Jerome Blitz (30) races toward the goal line to score on the game-opening kickoff versus the Princeton Tigers in 1952. The Crimson, however, lost the game 41-21.*

Opposite, inset: *QB Carroll Lowenstein threw for a school-record 258 yards against Princeton in 1950, but his strong passing wasn't enough to give the Crimson more than two victories that season.*

Rose Bowl. The resulting 44-0 pasting began a five-game losing streak for Harvard and 1-8 season. No Ivy opponents were beaten, and while the Boston media carried on a public debate about Harvard football's demise, Valpey forfeited the final year on his contract and became head coach at Connecticut.

In 1950, Lloyd Jordan took on the unenviable task of resuscitating Harvard football. Jordan's teams would be known for some of the greatest players in Harvard football history, but only three of his seven teams would be winners and, in the end, he failed to compile a winning mark against any Ivy League opponent. His first team lost its opening six contests and, in the first five of those, scored a single touchdown on four Saturdays and was blanked on the fifth. Finally the offense, and a diminutive passer named Carroll Lowenstein, emerged in a 63-26 rout by Dick Kazmaier and Princeton. The 145-pound Lowenstein threw for a school record 258 yards against the Tigers and, on the following week, fired touchdown strikes to Fred Ravreby and Gil O'Neil to lead Jordan to his first Harvard win, 14-13 over Brown.

That was Harvard's only win in 1950 and, if a two-year mark of 2-15 wasn't bad enough, the program took another blow, psychologically perhaps, when the steel stands that

closed the open end of Harvard Stadium were taken down in the summer of 1951. Extra seating had been needed when those stands were erected in 1929. That was no longer the case.

The 1951 season offered some hope as Lowenstein's passing was supplemented by the running of sophomore backs Dick Clasby and John Culver. However, Lowenstein was drafted by Uncle Sam and his replacement, Red Wylie, broke his arm. Still, the 3-5-1 record that followed was an improvement. A 22-21 win over Army was better than the 49-0 loss the year before. And a 21-21 tie in the season finale with Yale stopped a two-game losing streak in that series.

While team success was slow in developing, the period featured some tremendous individual efforts. In that 1951 Yale game, John Ederer ran 83 yards for a touchdown, the longest in the series' history to that point. In 1952, Clasby ran for 175 yards against Dartmouth and had a record 96-yard touchdown jaunt against Washington of St Louis. When Clasby hit Paul Crowley for a 42-yard touchdown pass against Princeton, it was the longest pass play for a touchdown against the Tigers in the history of that series and a mark that would stand until 1987. Clasby would go on to win nine letters at Harvard, three each in football, ice hockey, and baseball.

Other superlative efforts came from running back John Culver, later a U S Senator from Iowa. In the 1952 game with Springfield, Culver ran for 174 yards and three touchdowns. Jerry Blitz set a school mark by returning the opening kickoff against Princeton 93 yards for a touchdown. In all, 1952 saw a return of winning football to Cambridge after a five-year drought. The 5-4 mark gave Jordan the first of three straight winning seasons. Dick Clasby ran for 950 yards, a record that would last 30 years, and only the 41-14 shellacking by Yale at season's end ruined the party. That was the game in which Yale manager Charlie Yeager appeared and caught the pass which provided the Elis' final points.

The 1953 season featured Lowenstein, Clasby and Culver again and resulted in Jordan's best record, a 6-2 season blemished only by a pair of 6-0 Ivy losses to Columbia and Princeton. Following another winning campaign in 1954, the Jordan years closed quietly in 1955 and 1956. Such talented players as John Simourian, Matt Botsford, Jim Joslin, and Ted Metropoulos couldn't stem the tide. The 1955 season ended with a 21-7 loss to Yale, where the only points were scored when a kid named Ted Kennedy caught a touchdown pass. When Yale took the 1956 game by

42-14, Lloyd Jordan's career at Harvard came to a close.

If Jordan, out of Amherst, was an unlikely choice in 1950, what did Harvardians say when his successor came out of Gettysburg College? John Yovicsin would eventually seem very appropriate as head football coach at Harvard, but his first season was rough. 'Yovvy' never sought out the Harvard job. Former coach Dick Harlow had encouraged Harvard to seek out Yovicsin. And that's how the mild-mannered mentor arrived at Soldiers Field.

The 1957 season saw three wins in the first five weeks. But then things turned sour as the Crimson lost three straight, ending with 33-6 and 54-0 blowouts to Brown and Yale. The story goes that Yovvy was riding home after practice during that period when he was stopped for speeding by a suburban policeman. The officer looked at Yovicsin's license and said, 'Are you really John Yovicsin, the Harvard coach? You have enough problems,' and let the coach go.

There were mass defections from a troubled first team. In the end, only four seniors stayed on. (By contrast, Yovicsin's final team had 27 seniors.) Stressing defense, kicking, and then offense, Yovicsin molded solid – if not always exciting – winners. He was a man who taught fundamentals, ran the ball often, and relied heavily on a talented corps of assistant coaches. Many of his assistants went on to be head coaches elsewhere. Among the best were Foge Fazio (Pittsburgh), Jim Lentz (Bowdoin), Roger Robinson (Cortland), Pat Stark (Rochester), Alex Bell (Villanova) and Tom Stephens (Curry). Even one of his most celebrated captains became a coach, Vic Gatto '69 (Bates, Tufts and Davidson).

After two losing campaigns at the start, Yovicsin ran off a string of ten straight winning seasons. Before he retired following the 1970 season, John Yovicsin coached more seasons (14) and won more games (78) than anyone in Harvard history. He shared three Ivy League titles and won more than 60 percent of Ivy games and overall games.

The early Yovicsin teams featured hard-nosed players like Robert 'Shag' Shaunessy, a lineman who received honorable mention when the Ivy League selected a Silver Anniversary Team in 1981. There was running back Chet Boulris, as tough a player as Harvard ever had. Boulris was twice an All-Ivy performer and was named to the Team of the Decade when the tenth anniversary of formal league play was celebrated in 1966. Fullback Sam Halaby and split end Hank Keohane were

Opposite: *Tackle Robert 'Shag' Shaunessy served as team captain in 1959.*

Top: *The 1959 Crimson team went 6-3, losing only to Cornell, Dartmouth and Brown.*

Left: *The 1966 edition of the Crimson finished 6-1 for a three-way tie with Princeton and Dartmouth to top the Ivies.*

other notables of this period. When Boulris hit Keohane with an 85-yard touchdown pass against Yale in 1959, it established a Harvard record that still stands today. The 1959 team went 6-3 in a year that could easily have been perfect. Cornell's 20-16 win came on a 76-yard pass play with 24 seconds to go. Dartmouth won 9-0 in the mud. And Brown's 16-6 win was the result of a 40-yard interception returned for a touchdown and the Bruins' first field goal in ten years.

Six Yovicsin teams allowed fewer than 100 points in a season and, not surprisingly, the three teams that shared Ivy titles under Yovvy were among those six. The first shared title

came in 1961, a season where the loss of 16 key seniors was supposed to hurt the Harvards. That certainly seemed the case when the Crimson were 1-3 after four Saturdays. The only Ivy loss in that stretch was a costly 26-14 loss to Columbia. The rest of the season was Harvard's. Bill Grana had one touchdown and Bill Taylor added a pair as Harvard rebounded with a 21-15 over Dartmouth. Over the final four weeks of the season, the Crimson defense allowed a total of just 19 points en route to a 6-1 Ivy slate and a share of the crown with Columbia. Toughest foe in this stretch was Princeton, which fell 9-7.

Harvard lost just two Ivy games in each of

the next four seasons, but in none of those years was it enough for Ivy glory. Perhaps the most painful of these was 1963 when Harvard lost to Yale, 20-6, in a game postponed a week due to the assassination of President John F Kennedy '40. The President had attended the Columbia game at the Stadium earlier that year, and had in earlier seasons watched brothers Robert '48 and Edward '54 play varsity football for the Crimson.

The four years of near-misses for Harvard football came to an end in 1966 when the Crimson shared in the first three-way tie in league history. This was a season where everything came together for Harvard. Yovicsin's stingiest defense allowed just 60 points in nine games. Senior back Bobby Leo was closing out a brilliant career in which, among other things, he scored the winning touchdown in three straight Yale games. Sophomore back Vic Gatto complemented Leo and, of all things, Yovvy had a quarterback who could pass.

Lefthanded junior Ric Zimmerman would be Yovicsin's most prolific passing quarterback. He was the main reason that Harvard, which had scored just 120 points the year before, started 1966 with 109 points in just the first three weeks. After another week, Harvard was 4-0, had outscored the enemy 130-14, and faced a showdown with Dartmouth. The Big Green had a share of the last four Ivy championships and had a 10-game Ivy winning streak entering Harvard Stadium that day. But with Gatto and Leo running for 275 yards, and Zimmerman leading a seven-minute, 80-yard drive in the final minutes, Harvard rallied to defeat the Green, 19-14.

When it was Princeton driving 93 yards in the fourth quarter two weeks later, Harvard had its only league loss, 18-14. Harvard, Dartmouth and Princeton finished at 6-1 in the league in a year where Harvard outscored its opponents overall by 231-60, the widest margin since 1920.

In 1967, captain and linebacker Don Chiofaro led a team that produced a very respectable 6-3 record. But this squad will be best remembered for two games that got away, and its placement between two Ivy title years. The first of the painful losses came at the Stadium in October when Dartmouth came to town. Behind brilliant quarterback Gene Ryzewics, the visitors carried a 20-0 lead into the fourth quarter. Suddenly, Harvard's offense woke up, and behind a solo touchdown from Ray Hornblower and two from Vic Gatto, Harvard needed just seven minutes to take a 21-20 lead, with about eight minutes to play.

Dartmouth mounted a final drive and with

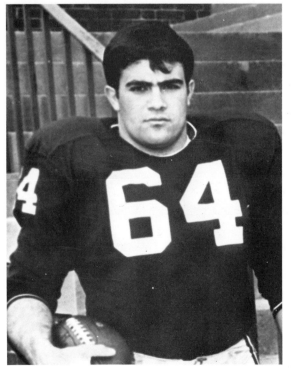

Opposite: *QB Ric Zimmerman calls the signals against Cornell in 1967.*

Above: *Halfback Vic Gatto was team captain in 1968.*

Left: *Linebacker Don Chiofaro was captain of the 1967 squad that went 6-3.*

1:07 left, and facing a fourth and six from the Harvard eight, the Green's Pete Donovan tried a game-winning field goal. The kick was wide left and the Harvard stands erupted. But they didn't see a flag on the play, one thrown for a Harvard offside violation. Donovan tried a second time and Dartmouth left the Stadium that day with a 23-21 win. (An eerily similar situation would occur in 1982 at the University of Pennsylvania.)

If that wasn't enough, the 1967 season finale at Yale provided even more pain for the Harvards. Trailing 17-0 against a team that would eventually go 7-0 in league play, Harvard battled back with 20 second-half points to take a 20-17 lead with three minutes left to play at the Yale Bowl. With 49 seconds remaining, Yale quarterback Brian Dowling connected on a 66-yard touchdown pass to Walt Marting, when a Harvard defender slipped on wet turf. It was then Yale, 24-20, on a day where the brilliant Dowling, before that toss, had had more passes caught by Harvard defenders (five interceptions) than by Yale receivers.

The Crimson got the ball back one more time, and in his final career moments, Ric Zimmerman moved the team to the Yale ten before a fumble killed the rally. After the game, Yovicsin told Zimmerman that no individual had done more for Harvard football in Yovicsin's eleven years than Zimmerman had. The pain

of that Yale game stayed with the returning Harvard football players. They had limited Dowling to five completions in 20 passes. They had played their hearts out. There would be atonement.

Much has been written about the 1968 Harvard team that started so inauspiciously. The season opener was a slim 27-20 verdict over non-league foe Holy Cross. Following a 59-0 destruction of Bucknell, the Ivy opener was a 21-14 win over Columbia. Then the defense came together. Players such as linebacker John Emery, safety Pat Conway and end Pete Hall keyed a defense that allowed just 27 points over the next five weeks. No opponent scored more than a touchdown in that stretch. And with Zimmerman's replacement, George Lalich, handing off to Gatto and Hornblower, and occasionally throwing to Bruce Freeman and Pete Varney, the offense was coming together too. One contributor on offense was a guard by the name of Tommy Lee Jones, later a

major motion picture star. Punter Gary Single-terry did his job so well that he would later receive honorable mention on the Silver Anni-versary Team.

Those next five Saturdays saw Cornell, Dartmouth, Pennsylvania, Princeton and Brown fall in succession. The toughest game in that stretch was a 9-7 squeaker at Princeton which, when followed by a 31-7 triumph over Brown, set up the first battle of perfect 8-0 teams in the 91 years since Harvard first met Yale, on 23 November 1968.

One has to understand the significance of any Harvard-Yale game to put this particular game in focus. Even without such historic weight, The Game is always special. It ends the season for the Harvards and the Yales. It changes seasons. When you enter The Game, it is fall. When you leave, it is winter. In 1968, it became a very cold winter for the people wear-ing blue.

Yale entered the game as a one-touchdown

Opposite top: Reserve QB Frank Champi (27) tosses a pass in the second quarter of the 1968 Yale game. His touchdown pass to Vic Gatto with three seconds to go followed by a PAT to Pete Varney gave the Harvards a wild 29-29 'win' over the Elis.

Opposite bottom: Coach John Yovicsin in 1969. In 14 seasons Yovvy amassed a 78-42-5 record.

Above: Sophomore QB Frank Champi (27), hero of the 1968 Yale defeat, gave up football the next year.

favorite. They had quarterback Dowling, who had never lost a game in either high school or college. They had a running back named Calvin Hill, later an NFL star with Dallas and Washington. The demand for tickets at Harvard was unprecedented. The game of the century was promised. But when Yale sped off to a 22-0 lead midway through the second quarter, at least half the 40,000-seat Stadium crowd was silent.

Late in the second quarter, in an effort to shake up his comatose offense, John Yovicsin lifted his undefeated quarterback Lalich and substituted sophomore Frank Champi. In his first possession, Champi moved the team 64 yards in 12 plays, ending with an eight-yard touchdown pass to split end Bruce Freeman. A bad snap botched Richie Szaro's kick attempt, and so the two teams left the field at halftime with Yale ahead, 22-6.

Lalich started the second half, but Harvard went nowhere. After a Yale fumble gave Har-

vard the ball, Champi returned to the lineup and three plays later, it was 22-13. Just as it appeared to be a game that might live up to its billing, Yale scored early in the fourth quarter and it was 29-13 for the visitors. With a 16-point lead behind a quarterback who had never lost a game in eight years, the Yale fans brought out white handkerchiefs and began waving them at the Harvard side of the field.

The lead could have been greater had Yale not fumbled five times. And on the Harvard side of the field, Hornblower was out with a bad ankle and Gatto, having pulled a hamstring early in the game, sat out most of the second half. Captain Gatto returned to the game late in the fourth quarter as another Yale fumble gave Harvard the ball with 3:31 to play. When Brian Dowling walked off the field to the Yale sideline, little did he know that his college football career was over. He never got a chance to touch the ball again. What happened next is part of college football history:

Time Remaining	Score	Ball On	Play
3:31	Y 29-13	H 14	– Champi pitches to Ballantyne. Loss of two.
			– Ballantyne gains 17 on reverse. First down. – Champi pass fails. – Champi sacked. Yale holding. First down. – Champi pass fails.
		Y 30	– Champi pass to Freeman good to Yale 30. First down. – Champi pass fails.
		Y 38	– Champi sacked. Third and 18 from Yale 38. – Champi back to pass, bobbles ball, laterals to tackle Fritz Reed who gains 23 yards. First down.
		Y 15	– Champi to Freeman. TD. – Champi to Varney for PAT incomplete. Yale called for interference.
		Y 1	– Crim from 1 for PAT.
0:42	Y 29-21		
		Y 49	– Harvard's Bill Kelly recovers onside kick. – Champi scrambles for 14. Yale called for face mask penalty. First down.
0:32	Y 29-21	Y 20	– Champi pass to Freeman fails. – Champi pass to Reynolds fails.
0:20	Y 29-21	Y 20	– Crim up middle for 14 (same play that Harvard fumbled on at end of 1967 game).
0:14	Y 29-21	Y 6	– Champi sacked at 8. Final time out.
0:03	Y 29-21	Y 8	– Champi to Gatto for touchdown.
0:00 0:00	Y 29-27 29-29	Y 3	– Champi to Varney for PAT.

Left: *QB Jim Stoeckel was one of the key members of Coach Joe Restic's multiflex offense in the early 1970s.*

Top: *John Yovicsin in 1969, his last year as head coach for the Crimson.*

Above: *Coach Joe Restic has a word with quarterback Larry Brown, who set new school single-season and career passing records in 1977 and 1978.*

Two quarterbacks, who had each led their teams to 8-0 records, watched the improbable ending to this improbable matchup from the sidelines. And in the end, as the *Harvard Crimson* would proclaim, Harvard 'beat' Yale, 29-29.

Yovicsin couldn't do anything for an encore. In fact, his 1969 team compiled the worst record of his 14-year Harvard career, 3-6. It was a season that began with the early retirement of Frank Champi and ended with a 7-0 loss at Yale. Said Champi at that time, 'Football has lost its meaning for me.' So the quiet backup who became part of Harvard athletic history for a fabled 42 seconds, walked away from the game two weeks into his junior year.

The Yovicsin era ended with a strong 7-2 record in 1970, after doctors convinced the coach to consider retirement. Yovvy had endured open heart surgery in 1965, and by 1970 the idle life seemed wiser. The coach went to work in Harvard's athletic department for a few years but then retired as he had arrived, quietly, to Cape Cod. His record, through 14 seasons, was 78-42-5. More importantly, he had restored the winning tradition to Harvard.

Records, it is said, are made to be broken. And so the man who replaced John Yovicsin would win more games over more seasons than even Yovvy. Joe Restic came to Harvard in 1971 with a reputation as an innovator. 'Defense wins games and offense pleases the crowd,' said Mr Restic upon arriving in Cambridge. That was before any of the Harvard faithful had ever heard the word 'Multiflex,' short for multiple and flexible, describing the offense that Restic had cultivated in his years as a college assistant and later as head coach of the Hamilton Tiger Cats in the Canadian Football League.

In that offense, the quarterback is the key. Restic would rely on one flexible, versatile athlete, often at the expense of having backup people ready. In some years, as in 1979 when five quarterbacks were lost, his strategy spelled disaster. But in general it was a success.

Restic's first team forged a 5-4 mark in 1971 and the jury stayed out late, stung by losses to archrivals Dartmouth and Princeton. But when Yale fell by 35-16, a few believers emerged. The next year, the team was 4-4-1 but 0-2-1 versus Dartmouth, Princeton and Yale (the tie was with the Green). And so alumni hesitated. Quarterback Jim Stoeckel was fun to watch running the offense, and Dave St Pierre was in charge of a good defense. But even when championships came Restic's way, the results against the major Ivy rivals would be thrown at him.

Above: *QB Jim Kubacki (19) scrambles in the 1975 Dartmouth game. He led the Crimson to the Ivy League title that season.*

Right: *QB Milt Holt, sporting his trademark white shoes, took the Harvards to a share of the Ivy League title in 1974.*

Opposite top: *Split end Pat McInally (84) on his way to a touchdown versus Holy Cross in 1979.*

Opposite bottom: *QB Larry Brown looks downfield for a receiver.*

In 1973, Restic appeared ready to close in on his first Ivy title. True, the Crimson had been tucked by Dartmouth, 24-18, making it five years without a win over the Hanoverians. But joy returned to Cambridge the following Saturday when Jim Stoeckel set records for completions (27), passes (48) and yards (291) in throwing Harvard to a 34-30 win at Pennsylvania. Ten of those passes went to split end Pat McInally whose final grab was a 30-yard touchdown with a minute and a half to go. The very next week, Restic fashioned his first win over Princeton, 19-14, and then watched his team come from behind to beat Brown, 35-32. With that, Harvard took a 7-1 record into the Yale Bowl for The Game. Rain and a fired-up Yale team proved to be no match for the visitors as the Elis prevailed, 35-0. Dartmouth won the Ivy title outright.

Restic would grab his first piece of the title the next year. Jim Stoeckel was gone, but a left-handed, white-shoed Hawaiian by the name of 'Pineapple' Milt Holt was there to take over.

Just as he would pitch Harvard's baseball team into the College World Series, Milt Holt threw the football well enough to get Harvard into first place. This would be a glorious season for Harvard fans. Holt was stylish, adaptable, and he had the irrepressible McInally at split end. Whether punting footballs or catching them, McInally was the league's best. And Holt was just what the Multiflex needed.

The turnaround game was at Dartmouth. With Joe Sciolla making a diving, game-saving pass deflection, the Crimson held on to a 17-15 win which broke the five-year jinx and kept Harvard on its championship schedule. With two weeks to go, Harvard was 6-1 overall, having lost to Rutgers by 24-21, and 5-0 in the league. Perhaps the squad was looking ahead to Yale, but the title express was derailed on the penultimate Saturday, 9-7 against Brown. Now it was 5-1 Harvard versus 6-0 Yale for a piece of the title.

The famed 1968 game might have had a flashy ending, but those who saw both still claim that the 1974 game was better from start to finish. Yale took advantage of four Harvard fumbles to go up 13-0 in the second quarter. Harvard came back behind two Holt touchdown tosses to take the lead, 14-13 at the half. It stayed that way until the fourth quarter when Yale capitalized on a bad snap in a punting situation to gain the ball and good field position. Settling for a field goal, Yale went ahead 16-14.

When Milt Holt took over for the last drive of his career, Harvard faced a first and ten on its own ten with just over five minutes to play. Nine runs, four complete passes and one incomplete pass later, Harvard faced a second and goal on the Yale one with a minute remaining. Holt and Restic's main concern was that Holt might get trapped on the field and time would expire. Holt called his own number and behind the blocks of Steve Dart and Tommy Winn, the white-shoed quarterback sprinted into the end zone for the win and share of the title. It was a fitting way for Harvard to celebrate 100 years of football, the 'real' centennial.

In 1975, Jim Kubacki took over quarterbacking duties for the Crimson. He was another lefthander, and another thinking man's quarterback. He could pass a little, he could run a little, and he could do both, quite frequently, in pain. Kubacki spent a good deal of time playing hurt, which makes his already-impressive numbers even more so. This would turn out to be another 7-2 season that saved the best for last.

Entering the final two games, Harvard was

Above: *Bill Emper (23) sails through the air to knock the ball away from Dartmouth's Jimmie Solomon, who waits with outstretched hands in the second quarter of the 1975 game. Harvard won.*

Right: *Tommy Winn (24) dives for a few more yards as he is tackled by Ed Backus of Columbia during first quarter action in 1976.*

Opposite top: *Coach Joe Restic monitors his team's performance from the sidelines.*

4-1, second only to 4-0-1 Brown. The task was simple: beat Brown and Yale, and Harvard has its first unshared Ivy championship. With Keith Jackson and an ABC-TV audience watching the happenings from Providence, Kubacki put on a show. Unable to practice all week, the quarterback was 13 of 15 for 222 yards in the first half alone. With Tommy Winn and Neal Miller providing the ground game, Harvard amassed 476 yards in total offense and won 45-26 before Brown's first sellout in 43 years.

That left Yale. The teams traded touchdowns through three quarters, which brought the game and the season down to the final drive. It was Winn and Miller running again, behind the blocks of captain Danny Jiggets, later a Chicago Bears regular. (Another future Bear, Gary Fencik, was Yale's key receiver who that day was held to a single reception by defensive back Bill Emper.) Kubacki had everything in gear. On a key fourth and 12, he

hit tight end Bob McDermott to keep the season's hopes alive. Finally, with 30 seconds to go, center Joe Antonellis snapped to holder Tim Davenport and kicker Mike Lynch tried a 26-yard field goal. With 65,000 Yale Bowl fans straining to follow its path, the ball cleared the uprights and Harvard had its Ivy League title.

The closing years of the 1970s couldn't maintain the excitement of 1974 and 1975. The 1976 squad was another winner at 6-3 but the rest of the decade trailed off at 4-5, 4-4-1, and 3-6. Standout of the 1977 and 1978 seasons was quarterback Larry Brown, as pure a passer as Harvard had ever seen. Like Holt, Brown was a star pitcher for the baseball team (he would later pitch in the Houston system). Brown twice passed for more than 300 yards and took over Harvard's season and career passing records.

The 1979 season was proof that it's not how many teams you beat but whom you beat that determines a successful season. This was the year of the injured quarterback. Five went down with injuries and so Harvard lost six straight after opening with two wins. Burke St John returned at quarterback for the season finale at Yale, where 8-0 Yale hosted 2-6 Harvard. Behind an inspired running game led by sophomore back Jim Callinan, Harvard kept it simple and stunned Yale, 22-7. To the Old Grads, this made it all acceptable.

Opposite: *QB Greg Gizzi gets good protection from Roger Caron (63) in 1984 action versus Yale.*

Above: *Bob Glatz (26) packs the pigskin for a big gain against Princeton in 1987.*

Far left: *QB Tom Yohe (7) heaves one downfield in 1987 action versus Princeton.*

Left: *Yohe runs the ball against Princeton in 1987. His superb performance that season brought the Crimson its second ever Ivy League championship.*

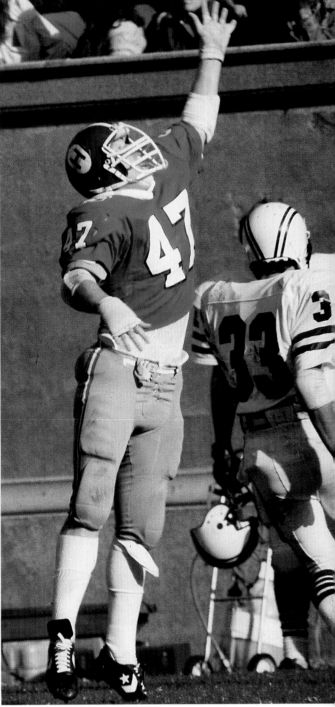

Callinan was the big story over the next two seasons as he assaulted the record books. The talented fullback became Harvard's first 1000-yard back when he ran for 1054 yards in 1981. In Callinan and defensive end Chuck Durst, Harvard had two All-Ivy performers who might have been stars on any Harvard team. But the 1980 and 1981 seasons were lacking; the records were 7-3 and 5-4-1 but the record against Dartmouth, Yale and Princeton was 0-5-1, and Yale claimed two shutouts.

Restic's critics were whispering again, but he produced a pair of shared titles in 1982 and 1983. The new Ivy power was Pennsylvania. Behind coach Jerry Berndt, the Quakers were recalling days of early success at Franklin Field. In 1982, Penn began a string of five straight titles, but the first was shared with both Harvard and Dartmouth. The Crimson offense in 1982 was in the hands of young Don Allard, son of a former Boston College and

New England Patriots quarterback. Allard emerged from the shadow of Ron Cuccia, a flashy Southern Californian who never quite lived up to his advance billing. Alternating with Cuccia at first, Allard took over when he threw for a record 358 yards in a 31-14 win over Massachusetts. When he led Harvard to successive wins over Princeton, Brown and Holy Cross, he became the leader that Restic was looking for.

On the next to last Saturday of the season, Allard led his team to Pennsylvania. The game was a carbon copy of the traumatic 1967 loss to Dartmouth. Penn went up 20-0, Harvard and Allard struck for three quick fourth-quarter scores to go up 21-20, and Penn came back with one last drive. They failed at a game-winning kick, received a second life after a penalty (roughing the kicker), and won the game when Dave Shulman's second try was good. But Penn lost to Cornell on the final

Opposite: *Mike McConnell (25) carries the ball in 1987 game action.*

Top left: *Record-breaking fullback Jim Callinan (32) jumps for joy after making a touchdown, 1980.*

Above: *Top running back Tony Hinz (47) makes a big reach for a high pass in 1986 action versus Dartmouth.*

Above: 'With the Crimson in triumph flashing/'Midst the strains of victory,/Poor Eli's hopes we are dashing/Into Blue obscurity!'

Right: 'Resistless our team sweeps goalward/ 'Midst the fury of the blast,/We'll fight for the name of Harvard/Till the last white line is passed!'

Far right: 'Ten thousand men of Harvard/Want victory today.'

Opposite: 'O'er the stands in flaming crimson,/Harvard banners fly.'

Above: *The Harvard defense holds back the Eli line in another chapter of one of football's greatest rivalries.*

Saturday when Harvard trounced Yale, 45-7, to end two years of whitewashing and grab a piece of the championship.

In 1983, a 2-2-1 start behind new quarterback Greg Gizzi left significant doubt as to Harvard's chances of repeating. But the team responded down the stretch, particularly on the final two weeks when Penn was blanked at the Stadium, 28-0, and stubborn Yale went down, 16-7, in the 100th playing of The Game. That victory left Harvard and Penn atop the league standings once more.

Three seasons went by before a full-scale run at the title could be mustered. And as had happened so many times in the past, the success came after difficulty. The 1986 team finished at 3-7, the first Restic team to have a losing record at home and on the road. The season did allow one star to emerge in Tom Yohe, the first sophomore to start at quarterback in seven years for Harvard.

Yohe began 1987 as the boss and he did so in style. Columbia, Northeastern and Bucknell fell as Yohe went to the air. At Cornell, Yohe

Left: *Cantab Jim Bell (93) takes out a Tiger in Big Three action.*

Below: *A Crimson and Green pileup during 1986 game action.*

threw for more than 200 yards for the third straight week, but it was a Big Red Hail Mary toss at game's end that gave the Ithacans the win. When Yohe threw for 200-plus yards in a 42-3 pummeling of Dartmouth, he became the first Harvard quarterback to do so for four straight weeks.

Next came Princeton. Restic was 6-8-2 against the Tigers and only twice in sixteen years had he been able to beat both Dartmouth and Princeton in the same year. With Yohe firing touchdown passes to Bob Glatz (48 yards) and Tony Hinz (40 yards), Harvard prevailed, 24-19, to stay in the Ivy race. Brown came next and was edged out by Harvard, 14-9, but when the Crimson came up against Holy Cross the next week they got a taste of serious football outside the Ivy League and went down 41-6. Penn was next and Harvard took them 31-14, leaving the Crimson to face only Yale – tied for first place in the Ivy League.

In a game played in bone-chilling weather, Harvard went into the third quarter down 10-7, when Tom Yohe connected with Tony Hinz; Harvard went ahead, 14-7, and held off a last-minute Yale rally to take the game and win the Ivy League – only its second unshared championship ever. Tom Yohe ended up owning a handful of Harvard career records with his passing, and since he had his senior year to come, it appeared that Harvard would continue its tradition as one of the perennial contenders for the Ivy League crown.

UNIVERSITY
OF
PENNSYLVANIA

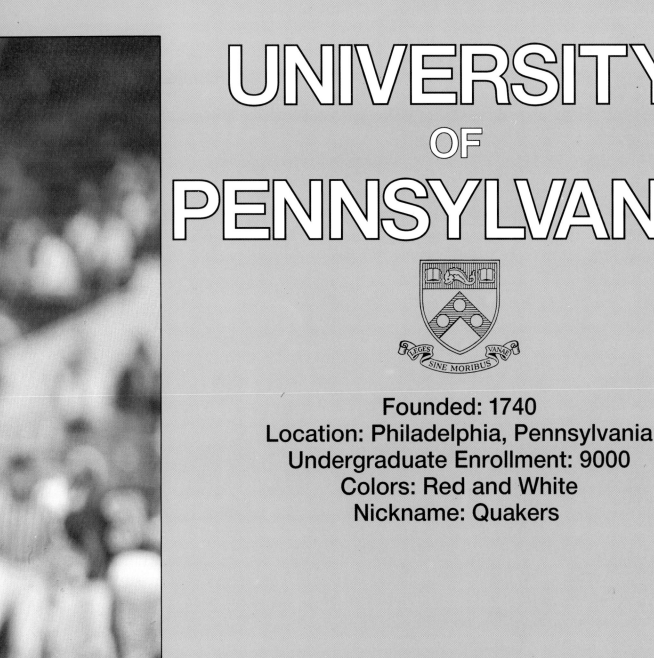

Founded: 1740
Location: Philadelphia, Pennsylvania
Undergraduate Enrollment: 9000
Colors: Red and White
Nickname: Quakers

HEWSON   F.M.DICK   S.JAMISON   L.C.BRASTOW   J.S.ELIOTT   C.C.THAYER   G.W.HUNT   G.T.HAZELHURST   H.H.LEE
                              W.M.STEWART   Captain   UMPIRE.
W.T.ROBINSON   J.T.BAILEY   E.A.WHITE   W.H.DRAYTON   A.M.HANCE   R.L.HART

*Previous pages: Penn
tackle Mike Lista and
linebacker Brad
Hippenstiel, both All-
Ivies, harry a Cornell
passer in 1987
competition.*

*Above: The fledgling
1878 team was the second
in Penn football history.*

Although the University of Pennsylvania made
an inauspicious debut in the football fraternity
that was to become the Ivy League with a 0-2-0
league record and 1-2-0 overall, it chose a most
appropriate year to embark on this All-
American sport: 1876. Appropriate not only
because Philadelphia was so closely involved
with the centennial celebrations that year but
because one of the school's founders was also
one of the nation's founders – Benjamin
Franklin. Begun in 1740 as a charity school, by
1755 it was the College and Academy of Philadelphia; it adopted its present name in 1791.
And because of their home city's strong ties
with the Society of Friends, Penn's team, in
their red and blue uniforms, is known as 'the
Quakers.'

Penn's football team did a little better in
1878, still with an 0-2-0 record in the league
but with an overall record of 1-2-1. Until 1894,
their total Ivy record was a meager 7-49-1,
although their overall tally was a bit better,
106-61-4. But 1894 was a miracle year. The
Quakers won all 12 of their games, three of
them against Ivy rivals. Unfortunately they
didn't win the league championship, because
Yale had won five Ivy games and had also gone
undefeated in 16 straight games. Penn did,
however, win the national championship in
1894, rolling up 304 points to its opponents'

20. Penn's winning streak eventually went to
34 in the next three years before Lafayette
broke it with a 6-4 win in 1896.

One of the major reasons for Penn's turnaround was George H Brooke, who ended up
playing six years of college football. After
being the Swarthmore fullback from 1889 to
1892, he played the same position for Penn in
1894 and 1895, making All-America twice, the
first time when he was only 19 years old.
Besides being a runner, he also did the kicking
for the Quakers. The term 'coffin corner kick'
was first applied to Brooke's slanting punts,
which rolled out of bounds close to the angle
formed by the sidelines and the goal line and
left the opponent in difficult field position.

Two other important factors on the superb
1894 team were Charles S Gelbert and Dana
'Win' Winchester. Gelbert, a deadly tackler
who weighed only 160 pounds, played both
guard and end. He was voted All-American
that year. Winchester, who had started out at
Cornell in 1891 and 1892, transferred to Penn
for the 1893 and 1894 seasons. A smooth,
effortless runner, he carried the Quakers to a
24-3 record in those two years, and helped the
Quakers score 850 points against their opponents' 82.

Penn finally won the Ivy title in 1895, winning three games in the league (outscoring

J.H.MINDS   O.WAGONHURST   BLAIR   W.T.WORTH   F.DELAGARRE   A.E.BULL   M.G.ROSENGARTEN   G.H.BROOKE   J.B.STA---
C.S.GELBERT   W.D.OSGOOD   A.A.KNIPE   AIKEN   C.L.UPTON
                                      CAPTAIN   C.S.WILLIAMS

Above: *The 1894 team rose above an early mediocre Penn record to win all 12 of their games. Notables include Charles Gelbert (first row, far left), George Brooke (second row, second from right), Jack Minds (second row, second from left), QB and later Penn coach Carl Williams (third row, second from left), and Buck Wharton (third row, first on left).*

Right: *Penn's Charles Gelbert, the 'miracle man' whose 160-pound frame belied his tackling clout as end and guard.*

Far right: *Penn guard Charles 'Buck' Wharton (1893-96) was All-America in 1895, the season that Penn took first in the Ivies and scored 480 points to 24 on the national level.*

their opponents 75-16), and 14 straight games overall, scoring 480 points to their opponents' 24. One of the stars of the year was Charles 'Buck' Wharton who, under Coach George Woodruff, played from 1893 to 1896. A guard who stood 6-feet 1-inch and weighed 235 pounds, Wharton made the All-America team in 1895 and 1896. While he was in Philadelphia, the Quakers won 52 of 56 games.

John Henry Minds played for Penn from 1894 to 1897 and starred while the Quakers were going 51-1. A versatile player, he saw service as a tackle, end, defensive guard, halfback

and fullback, and was team captain in 1897. He carried on George Brooke's tradition as a kicker by using the coffin-corner kick, often punting on the run. He made the All-America team in 1897.

Pennsylvania came back to win the Ivy title again in 1896, going 4-0-0 in the league and 14-1-0 overall, scoring 324 points to their opponents' 24. In addition to Minds, one of the stars was T Truxton Hare, who made the All-America team four times from 1897 to 1900. A guard, he played all 60 minutes in every game (55) in the four years he was at Penn. While he was there, the Quakers went 48-5-2 and shut out their foes 33 times. On the occasion of the centennial of college football in 1969, Hare was picked as the best guard of football's first 50 years, along with Pudge Heffelfinger of Yale. Besides being the captain of the team in 1899 and 1900, Hare was also an IC4A point-winning hammer thrower, and finished second in the hammer at the 1900 Olympics in Paris.

Penn's coach in this period, George W Woodruff, was a Yale graduate. He coached at Lehigh before taking the helm in Philadelphia from 1892 to 1901, and turned Penn into co-national champions in 1894, 1895 and 1897. His ten-year record was 124-15-2, and his teams scored 1777 points to its opponents' 88.

Although the 1904 team could only manage a tie for the Ivy title with Yale (they both went 4-0 and neither gave up a point to their opponents), the Quakers did once again tie for the national championship, by going undefeated in 12 games and scoring 222 points while giving up only four. After leading Penn to 12 straight victories, Vincent Stevenson, the 142-pound quarterback, was elected to the All-America team. The legendary Walter Camp said of him, 'He has all the requisites of a good quarterback, including his ability to handle punts. In directing the plays he steadies the team. He is fearless, he's imaginative, he's a fighter.'

Dr Carl Williams was the coach of the 1904 team. He had been the captain of the 1895 Quakers, and had succeeded George Woodruff in 1902. During that magic 1904 season, Penn defeated Brown (6-0), Columbia (16-0), Harvard (11-0) and Cornell (34-0). Three members of the team were on the first-string All-America team, two on the second team, and two on the third team. George Trevor of *The New York Times*, wrote:

If I were compelled to pick the greatest of all Penn elevens, I would name Captain [Bob] Torrey's 1904 juggernaut. A stonewall on defense, allowing its opponents one paltry field goal, Torrey's team packed the hardest punch in Pennsylvania's history. Despite the strength of the opposition, no rival crossed Penn's goal in 1904. They couldn't dent the line. Rough-and-tumble Bob Torrey, a born scrapper, originated the roving style of center play. He was the first center to play loose behind the line on defense. In the backfield, Vincent Stevenson had no equal at quarterback. A hard-bitten merciless driver whose tongue stung like a scorpion, he electrified players and spectators by his blood-chilling flying hurdles. He would leap high in the air when cornered, legs lashing out sideways like scythes. Harold Weekes of Columbia was the first exponent of the flying hurdle, but he employed it to scale the line of scrimmage, whereas Stevenson's breathtaking leaps were executed on the dead run in the open field.

Stevenson's leaping eventually led to the rules committee's legislation against hurdling.

Carl Williams had another unbeaten team in 1905, but this schedule included a 6-6 tie with Lafayette, which broke Penn's 20-game winning streak. Once again the Quakers had to settle for a tie in the Ivies with Yale. Both of them went 4-0. Bob Torrey, after being elected to the third team All-America in 1904, made the first team in 1905.

Between 1907 and 1910, the Quakers had some of their finest teams, going 38-3-4. Even though the 1908 club went 11-0 and again became the national co-champion, it did not win the Ivy title. Harvard took the crown with

Above: *Penn coach George Woodruff (1892-1901), former guard at Yale, racked up a remarkable 124-15-2 record.*

Below: *Quaker QB Vincent Stevenson with the ball in the 1904 shutout of Harvard, 11-0.*

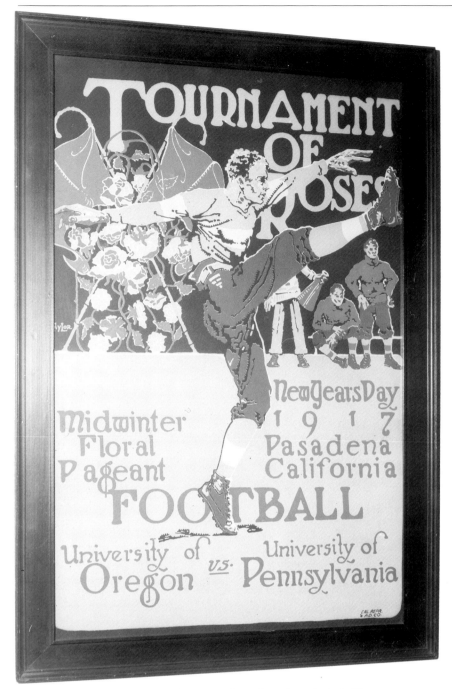

gether. Yale's Pudge Heffelfinger said of him, 'I doubt if the game of football has ever seen a tougher man than the roughhouse, hard-nosed Bill Hollenback. So help me, he actually played one game with a slight fracture of the leg and shrugged off such minor injuries as shoulder separations, shin splints and hip bruises. He was indestructible.' Hollenback played from 1904 to 1908, thus opening and closing his career on national championship teams. He later went on to coach at Penn State, Missouri, Pennsylvania Military College and Syracuse.

Pennsylvania won the Ivy championship in 1910. They only had a 2-0 record in the league, but that was enough. The Quakers went 9-1-1 that year overall, and held their opponents to a measly 14 points while scoring 184. The star of the team was LeRoy E Mercer, who played fullback from 1910 to 1912, and was the captain in 1911 and 1912. During his career under Coach Andy Smith, he was also on the 1912 United States Olympic team in Stockholm, and won the IC4A broad jump title.

Nineteen seventeen was a strange year. Penn went only 2-0 in the Ivy Group, but that was enough to win the championship, since only Brown, with a 1-0 record, won any games in the league. With World War I looming, only these two teams, plus Cornell and Dartmouth, had not gone to informal scheduling. The Quakers had a 9-2 season, and went to the Rose Bowl, where they were defeated by the University of Oregon, 14-0.

John William Heisman, the man after whom the Heisman Trophy was named, had played center, tackle and end for Penn in 1890 and 1891, and he came back to coach at his alma mater from 1920 to 1922. He was a peripatetic coach, and in his career, in addition to the Quakers, he coached at Oberlin, Akron, Auburn, Clemson, Georgia Tech, Washington and Jefferson, and Rice. His 185-70-17 record makes him one of the most successful coaches of all time. He traditionally faced his recruits at the beginning of a football season holding a football in his hands and saying, 'What is it? A prolate spheroid, an elongated sphere, one in which the outer leathern casing is drawn up tightly over a somewhat smaller tubing.' Then, after a pause, 'Better to have died as a small boy than to fumble this football.'

In 1924 Penn was not only the champion of the Ivies with its 2-0 record, but also the champion of the East with a 9-1-1 mark. They scored 203 points to their opponents' 31. That was the last year Walter Camp prepared his All-America list, and he picked tackle Ed McGinley of Penn to his first team.

In 1925, the Quakers had a 7-2 record, but

a 4-0 record against Penn's 3-0. The team went 11-0-1 and scored 215 points against its opponents' 18. Sol Metzger, who had been captain of the 1903 team, was the coach, and All-American Bill Hollenback was the captain. That was also the year that Penn throttled the University of Michigan, 29-0, even though Michigan had Hall of Famer 'Germany' Schulz at center. After the game, Michigan coach Fielding Yost said, 'Penn deserves being rated over Harvard as the nation's top team.'

One of the stars on that 1908 team that shared the national championship with the University of Chicago was end Hunter Scarlett, who played for the Quakers from 1905 to 1908. His teammate, Bill Hollenback, called him 'one of college football's greatest ends. He's a superlative defensive end, quick to get downfield on punts, and an exceptional diagnostitian.'

But it was Hollenback who held the team to-

Left: In the memorable 1940 Thanksgiving Day game Gene Davis's field goal from the 28-yard line at the end of the first half gave Penn the halftime lead over Cornell 16-13. Penn went on to win 22-20.

Below: Rejoicing Penn coach George Munger flanked by the stars of the 1940 come-from-behind win over Cornell. Center Ray Frick (left) intercepted three passes. Running back Frank Reagan's remarkable head-first smash at the five-yard line gained his third and winning TD and lost him two of his teeth.

went 3-0 in the Ivies, enough to tie Dartmouth, with an identical record, for the championship. The Quakers outscored their opponents 165-64 and had even beaten the mighty University of Chicago team. But then the University of Illinois invaded Franklin Field, bringing along the legendary Harold 'Red' Grange. 'The Galloping Ghost' scored three touchdowns and ran for 363 yards in 36 tries as the Illini won, 24-2. Except for that game, Penn would have outscored its opponents by 163-40.

Penn's next Ivy championship was in 1928, when they were 3-0 in the league and 8-1 overall, scoring 271 points to their opponents' 26. The Quakers repeated in 1929, going 2-0 and 7-2. The 1930s were not kind to Penn. In 1930 and 1931, they were 0-1 in the league, but 11-4 overall. They came in second to Brown in 1932 with a 2-0 record (Brown was 3-0) but slipped to 0-2 in 1933 and 1-2 in 1934. They broke even in 1935 with a 2-2 record, and came in third in 1936 with a 3-1 behind Dartmouth (5-0) and Yale (5-1). The next year, 1937, was another disaster – no league wins and 2-5-1 overall. Things began to get better in 1938 (2-1-1 in the league, and 3-2-3 overall) and 1939 (2-1-1 and 4-4).

The 1940s were probably the greatest decade in Penn football history, with George Munger as the coach from 1938 to 1953. In seven of the ten seasons of the 1940s, Penn did not lose an Ivy League game, going 38-3-2 for the decade, and 57-21-4 overall. They won the title in 1940, 1941, 1942, 1943, 1945 and 1947. During this time they were also playing such powers as Army, Navy, Michigan, Maryland, Virginia, Penn State and Pittsburgh.

One of the most outstanding games of the decade for Penn was the 1940 contest against Cornell at Franklin Field, with 80,000 enthusiastic fans in attendance. Cornell had been the Ivy League champion during the previous two years. In 1940, however, the Quakers had beaten Ohio State, 21-7, the second straight year they had done this, and lost to Michigan, whose star was the legendary Tom Harmon, by only 14-0. They had also beaten Army, 48-0, and Yale, 50-7.

The star of the Cornell game was Frank Reagan, the great runner. He had been recruited by almost every major college in the East, but Penn got him. In the game, Cornell leaped off to a 13-0 lead. But then captain and center Ray Frick of Penn intercepted a pass and ran it to the ten. It took Reagan four plunges, but he scored. Reagan came back with another touchdown and the score was tied, 13-13. Just before the end of the half, quarterback Gene

Davis kicked a field goal, and Penn was ahead, 16-13. In the third quarter, Cornell scored a touchdown to take the lead, 20-16, but Reagan marched the ball down the field in the last four minutes of the game, running from the Cornell 16 for a touchdown. The final score was Penn 22, Cornell 20. The Quakers went on to post a 6-1-1 for the 1940 season and win the league championship with a 3-0-1 record.

In 1947, Penn had its first undefeated team since 1908. They did suffer a tie with Army, 7-7, but they beat Lafayette, Dartmouth, Columbia, Navy, Princeton, Virginia and Cornell. They scored 219 points against their opponents' 35. The stars of the team were center Chuck Bednarik, back Skippy Minisi and tackle George Savitsky.

Charles 'Chuck' Bednarik was voted the greatest center of all time in 1969 by a prominent panel of coaches, writers, Hall of Fame players and football historians. He played from 1945 to 1948 and was twice voted to the

Below: *The soft-spoken Coach Munger inspired Penn teams from 1938 to 1953 to win 56 of their 62 Ivy games, taking the unofficial Ivy title nine times and standing up to such powerhouse teams as Army, Navy, Michigan and Notre Dame.*

Right: *When coach Steve Sebo took over in 1954 he had the problem of adhering to Ivy restrictions while facing rivals who had no such limitations. Soon after Penn football fell into a slump, losing 19 consecutive games.*

Below: *In the last game of 1959 the Quakers' Barney Berlinger snatches a pass from George Koval in Cornell's end zone, giving Penn the lead and the momentum to win 28-13.*

Opposite: *The legendary Penn center Chuck Bednarik in 1948 was the All-America choice of just about every judge in the country. A member of the Football Hall of Fame, Bednarik has been called the greatest center in history.*

All-America squad. This 6-foot 3-inch, 235-pound all-star was a two-way, 60-minute performer even though free substitution was allowed at the time. He had come to college after serving with the United States Army Air Corps as an aerial gunner during World War II. During his varsity career, the 'Bethlehem Bomber' led the Quakers to 24 wins in 27 games, and won the Maxwell Award in his senior year. In 1948 he was the number one draft choice in the National Football League, and played with the Philadelphia Eagles from 1949 through 1960.

Penn's greatest year during the 1950s was 1952. The Quakers won the Ivy title by going undefeated in the league, beating Dartmouth, Princeton, Columbia and Cornell. In addition, they tied Notre Dame and Navy and lost to Penn State, Georgia and Navy. This was the year when Penn broke Princeton's 24-game winning streak. After the 1953 football season, George Munger announced his retirement as head coach of the Quakers, ending his career with an 82-42-10 record.

In 1959, Coach Steve Sebo and his team had come off a 4-5-0 season, and were not expected to do much. But the Quakers stunned Lafayette (26-0), Dartmouth (13-0), Princeton (18-0) and Brown (36-9). Next they played Navy to a 22-22 tie. After a 12-0 loss to Harvard, they beat Yale, 28-12, and Columbia, 24-6. That brought them down to the final game of the season against Cornell. Cornell jumped to a 13-0 lead, but substitute George Koval bailed the Quakers out in a 28-13 vic-

tory to win the Ivy League championship.

Even though he had brought the school this title, Sebo had coached his last game at Penn. In 1960 Penn was touted as a possible winner. After Sebo had been fired, John Stiegman came over from Rutgers and tried to install a single wing formation. George Koval, who had been the long-throwing quarterback the year before, was switched to tailback. The Quakers struggled to avoid last place until the final game of the year against Cornell, a team also trying to stay out of the cellar. Koval was finally used as a passer, with Stiegman shifting him in and out of all the backfield positions, confusing the Big Red. Penn won, 18-7, which gave them a 2-5 league mark, good enough for sixth place.

That year was the beginning of a long period in the doldrums for Pennsylvania, and they were to go until 1968 before they climbed out of the second division of the league. They fell to seventh place in 1961, winning only one league game out of seven, and being outscored by the other Ivies 22-167. The Quakers clawed their way back to sixth in 1962, going 2-5 in the league and 3-6 overall. Then came two straight years in the cellar – 1963 and 1964, with league records of 1-6 and 0-7 respectively. Their overall record those two years was 4-14, and they were outscored by 145-411. Penn was in sixth place in 1965, seventh in 1966, and sixth in 1967. During those three years they won but five league games while dropping 15 and tying one, being outscored 532 to 328.

The Quakers rose to third place in 1968, with a league record of 5-2 and a 7-2 overall. It was like old times on the final day of the season. Penn had lost only to Yale and Harvard (the co-champions) and faced Dartmouth in front of 50,188 fans in Franklin Field. Quarterback Bernie Zbrzeznj passed for 176 yards and fullback Gerry Santini ran for 133 yards, and the Quakers beat the Indians, 26-21.

Then it was back to the second division for three more years, as Penn finished fifth in 1969 (with a 2-5 league record and 4-5 overall), sixth in 1970 (2-5, 4-5) and seventh in 1971 (1-6, 2-7). In 1972, Penn was tied with Cornell for third place, finishing behind Dartmouth and Yale. The highlight of the season was the Harvard game. Adolph Bellizeare ran 80 yards for a touchdown on the first play from scrimmage, ending up with a total of 203 yards overall for the Quakers. Penn scored 29 points in the second half to beat Harvard, 38-27. Not only was this the first win over the Crimson in nine seasons, it was the most points scored by Penn against Harvard since 1881.

The next year, 1973, the Quakers tied for

Above: *Penn closes in on a Princeton back in a 1968 game in which the Quakers beat the Tigers for the first time since 1959.*

Left: *Adolph 'Beep Beep' Bellizeare (6) trying to break through traffic on the grid with Princeton in 1972. His spectacular running style and yardage made him Penn's all-time leading rusher.*

second place with Harvard and Yale (with 5-2 records) as Dartmouth finished first at 6-1. Once again, 'Beep Beep' Bellizeare was the star of the team, racing for 849 yards and 11 touchdowns. It was back to third place in 1974; although Penn finished with a 4-2-1 record in the league, they were outscored 154-122. In 1975, Penn sank to sixth place (tied with Columbia, each 2-5); in 1976, Penn managed a tie for fifth place with Cornell, Princeton and Columbia (all 2-5); Penn came back to third place in 1977 (tied with Dartmouth and Harvard, all 4-3); and then they collapsed to eighth both in 1978 (1-5-1) and 1979 (0-7), seventh in 1980 (1-6), and eighth in 1981 (1-6).

Then, wonder of wonders, Penn did a complete about-face to become the scourge of the Ivy League for the next several years. (Only in 1987 was it publicly revealed that, as a special 'lifebelt' to keep Penn's football program from sinking forever, the other Ivy League schools had allowed Penn to relax their admissions policies slightly below league standards to recruit some players – the same lifebelt the league would throw Columbia when its team hit an all-time low a few years later.) In 1982, Penn suddenly appeared in a tie for first place with Dartmouth and Harvard; only an upset by Cornell in the last game of the season prevented Penn from taking first by itself. Penn also ended up in first place in 1983, this time tied with Harvard; Penn pulled this off by defeating Dartmouth in the last game of the season, 38-14, scoring 21 of their points in one

five-and-a-half-minute stretch; the star was senior fullback Chuck Nolan, who gained 130 yards rushing and scored two touchdowns.

In 1984, Penn defeated all its Ivy League rivals and took over the title by itself – the first time Penn had done this since 1959. In 1985, Penn lost to Harvard but still went on to take first place in the league all by itself after barely defeating Dartmouth, 19-14, in the final game of the season. Stars for the offense in 1985 were Mike O'Neill and Jim Bruni, while defensive standouts included Tom Gilmore – also winner of the Bushnell Cup – and Jeff Fortna.

The best was yet to come, though, when in 1986 Penn not only defeated all its Ivy League opponents but also three other teams (Bucknell, Lafayette and Navy) for its first perfect season since 1904. Ed Zubrow had replaced Jerry Berndt as head coach only this season and had inherited a remarkable group of players. Rich Comizio led the league in yards gained rushing (769) while Chris Flynn was third (with 738) and led in touchdowns scored (10). Jim Crocicchia was another standout, with a total of 1200 yards gained passing (879 in league games). On the defensive team, Bruce McConnell, A J Sebastianelli, Jeff Fortna, Mike Lista, Dexter Desir, Brad Hippenstiel, Jim Fangmeyer, and Donald Wilson were the strongmen. The team's test came in the final game of the season when they came up against Cornell, also undefeated in league play, and defeated them, 31-21.

The 1987 season began with Penn's having

Above: *A free-for-all ball between Penn and Dartmouth in 1983. That season Penn again tied with Harvard for first place and would hold the championship for the next three years.*

Opposite: *Penn's Jerry McFadden (77) and Bill Lista (53) sack the Harvard QB in a 1982 game. Penn's 1982 season dramatically reversed the 1981 team's lowly place with a Penn-Dartmouth-Harvard Ivy title.*

Right: *Quakers go in for the plunder after Mike Lista made the first hit on a Navy ball-carrier in 1987.*

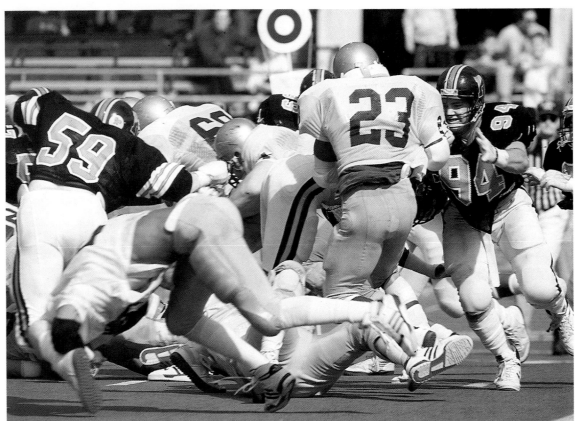

Right: *Penn LB Brad Hippenstiel records a sack versus Brown.*

Below: *Penn's Chris Flynn turns the corner versus Cornell.*

Above: *Penn tackle Eric Poderys (98) comes up to make a hit on a Columbia runner in 1987 game action.*

Right: *Quaker Brian Keys (4) goes up the Dartmouth middle in the final game of the 1987 season.*

Above: *Penn's excellent defense sacks the Dartmouth QB in 1987 action.*

Opposite: *Penn defensive end Scott Chandler turns the ball upfield after an interception versus Dartmouth. The Quakers closed their 1987 3-4 season with some cheer as they ended this game in a 49-7 rout of the Green.*

lost 15 starters from the unbeaten team of 1986, but plenty of talent remained and the experts were expecting another great year. After all, Penn had lost only four Ivy League games in its last 35. Back Chris Flynn was expected to win the Asa Bushnell Cup as the top player in the league, and Jim Bruni, a talented tailback, was trying his hand at fullback. Also returning was Brent Novoselsky, an All-Ivy tight end. On defense, All-Ivies Mike Lista (tackle), Brad Hippenstiel (linebacker) and Don Wilson (cornerback) were returning to the squad. The only gap that the Quakers seemed to have was at quarterback. A winning season seemed to be virtually inevitable.

It was expected that the opening game against Cornell might decide the Ivy League championship. Penn disappointed its fans by dropping the contest, 17-13, at Franklin Field, thus ending its 11-game winning streak and its eight consecutive Ivy wins at home. The second game of the season was even worse, as the Quakers were beaten by lowly Bucknell, 32-24. But the Quakers came back and took the next two games, against Columbia and Brown, only to lose the following three – to Navy, Yale and Princeton. They got back on track the next Saturday by beating Lafayette, but then fell to Harvard (the eventual Ivy League champion).

The Quakers' final game of the 1987 season was a whopping 49-7 victory over Dartmouth, in which Chris Flynn ran for 194 yards and five touchdowns for Penn. The year ended on this upbeat note, despite the Quakers' 3-4 finish in the Ivy League and 4-6 overall, their first losing season since 1981. But no one doubted, least of all their fellow Ivy Leaguers, that Penn's football team would be back for more in the years ahead.

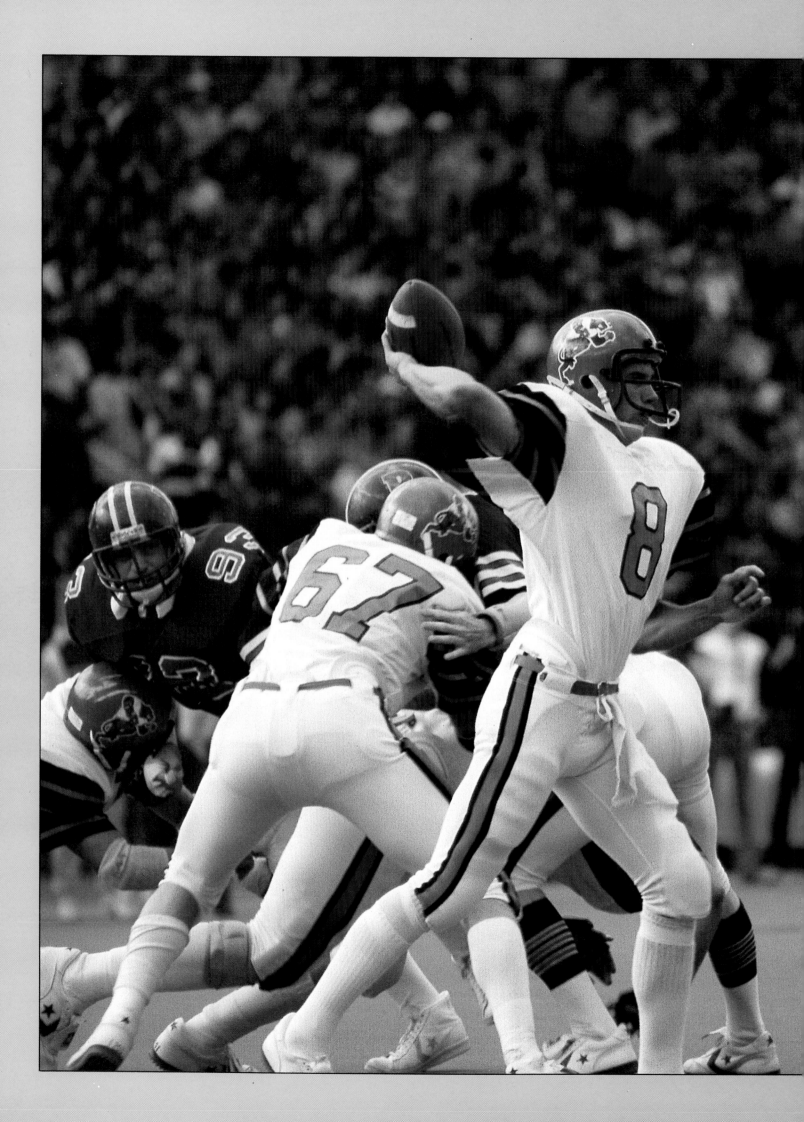

PRINCETON UNIVERSITY

Founded: 1746
Location: Princeton, New Jersey
Undergraduate Enrollment: 4500
Colors: Orange and Black
Nickname: Tigers

Previous pages: *Tiger Doug Butler (9) heaves one downfield against the Quakers.*

Above: *A painting by W N Boyd depicting the first intercollegiate football game, played between Princeton and Rutgers in New Brunswick, New Jersey, on 6 November 1869.*

Top right: *A plaque at Rutgers commemorating the first intercollegiate football game, which was played on the Rutgers campus.*

Right: *A drawing by A B Frost of the football match between Princeton and Yale on 27 November 1879.*

Princeton can lay claim to many fine traditions, both on and off the gridiron. To begin with, it is the fourth oldest university in the United States – only Harvard, William and Mary, and Yale are older. Founded in 1746 as The College of New Jersey, the institution was granted a royal charter from King George II of England. It was originally established by the Presbyterian Church at Elizabeth, New Jersey, and classes began in 1747 at the home of the Reverend Jonathan Dickson, the school's first president. After Dickson died, the college was moved to Newark in 1748 and to Princeton in 1756. The name of the school was not changed to Princeton University until 1896.

The college also holds a special place in the history of football in the United States. The school that was to become Princeton Univer-

sity was there when America's college football game was born in 1869. Nearby Rutgers College was still steaming over its baseball game with The College of New Jersey three years before, when the 'Princeton Bloods' had thrashed them, 40-2. Revenge in the form of a football game seemed to be the answer. So Rutgers sent a 'defiant but courteous' written challenge to the men of Nassau Hall to engage in a football contest. The challenge was accepted, Old Nassau formed a team, and William S Gummere, Class of 1870, was elected captain.

The first intercollegiate football game began at three o'clock on 6 November 1869, in New

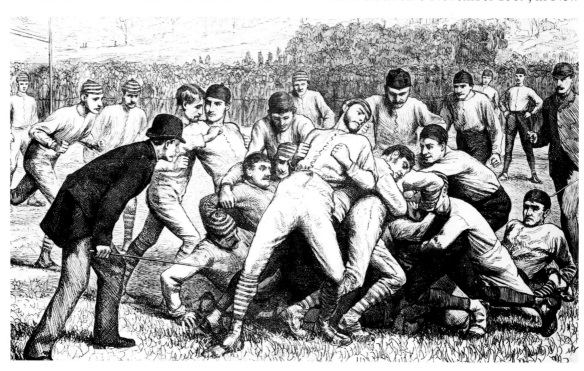

Brunswick, New Jersey, the site of Rutgers University. The players wore the letters 'P' and 'R' on the chest of their turtleneck sweaters, the 'P' standing for 'Princeton Bloods.' In a game played more like soccer than modern football, Rutgers won, 6 goals to 4. A week later, the same two teams met in a rematch and The College of New Jersey won, 8-0. Thus ended the first season of college football, with the only teams in the country tied for the national championship with one win and one loss each.

When the first formal rules for the game of football were adopted at a meeting in New York City on 19 October 1873, The College of New Jersey had a place on the rules committee, along with representatives from Yale, Rutgers and Columbia. The first forward pass was thrown during the Yale game of 1876. Yale's Walter Camp, who was to go on to become the 'father of college football,' was being tackled by Nassau Hall players when he threw the ball to Oliver Thompson, who ran it in for a touchdown. Of course the Old Nassau players protested this completely unorthodox maneuver, but Yale countered by pointing out that there

were no rules against it. The confused umpire decided to toss a coin in order to make a decision, and the touchdown stood.

In 1877 the boys from Princeton took the field wearing the first college football uniforms. Created by a Nassau player, L P Smock, they included a jersey with an orange 'P,' a tight canvas jacket, black knee pants and stockings. Thus the team would soon earn the nickname, the Tigers. By 1878 the league had blossomed to six teams (only Dartmouth and Cornell of the present Ivy League were not included), and Old Nassau won all four of its league games for the league championship, going undefeated with two outside wins to boot. This was the year of the first big college football crowd, when The College of New Jersey played Yale in front of 4000 fans in Hoboken, New Jersey. The $300 paid to rent the field was considered extravagant.

Old Nassau again won the league championship in 1879, finishing with a 3-0-1 record and going 4-0-1 overall. Then in 1880 they beat Columbia, 1-0, in the first college football game ever to be forfeited. Another championship came in 1881, when The College of New

Above: *The 1873 Princeton team chose to wear formal attire for the shooting of their team photo.*

Above: *This illustration shows well-dressed spectators observing the Princeton-Yale match at the Berkeley Oval in 1889.*

Jersey finished 3-0-2 in the league, with a 7-0-2 overall record. This was the year that the first intersectional college football games were played, when the University of Michigan came East to play Yale, Harvard and Old Nassau and lost, of course, to the Orange and Black.

Alex Moffat of the Tigers was college football's first great kicker. It was he who invented the spiral punt in 1881, and it changed the whole science of punting. He may well have been the best dropkicker of all time. In 1883, the year he was captain of the team, he kicked five field goals against Harvard – two of them right-footed, two of them left-footed and one from placement. That was also his best year overall – he kicked 16 field goals, seven extra points and scored seven touchdowns.

In 1884 Yale and Old Nassau tied for the league championship, each with 2-0-1 records. They were both powerhouses, with the Orange and Black posting an overall 9-0-1 total and Yale an 8-0-1. This was the year that the Tigers first used the V-trick, or wedge, against the University of Pennsylvania. In games of that era, the two teams lined up ten yards apart at the kickoff. In the Penn game, the Tigers' kicker nudged the ball ahead while his team-mates formed a V-shaped wedge, providing interference as the kicker moved the ball along.

In 1885 the Tigers once again went undefeated, compiling a 9-0-1 overall record and going 4-0-0 in the conference. The highlight of the season was probably the Yale game. Yale was leading, 5-0, with one minute to go. Then Tiger Tilly Lamar picked up a bounding punt and ran 80 yards through the whole Yale team to score a touchdown. The final score: Orange and Black 6, Elis 5.

On the first list of All-America players, compiled in 1889 by Caspar Whitney of *Harper's Weekly* (with a lot of help from Walter Camp), there was a Princeton man named Edgar Allan Poe – the grandnephew of the poet. He was the captain in 1889 and 1890, and in the Penn game of 1890 he became the first player ever to use a rubber nose guard, to protect a broken nose. The Yale great, Pudge Heffelfinger, once said of him, 'You'd knock him down and he'd bounce back up again. He recoiled like a highly sensitive spring. Again and again he struck, endlessly, wearing us out. He handled our ball carriers as though they were wooden soldiers.' Yet Poe weighed less than 155 pounds. John P Poe, the father of Edgar Allan and the nephew of the poet, would furnish the Orange and Black with six sons who were to become outstanding football players. In addition to Edgar Allan (Class of 1891), there were S Johnson ('94), John P, Jr ('95), Nielson ('97), Arthur ('00) and Gresham ('02).

The Tigers dominated the 1889 All-America list, placing six of the 11 players on it. In addition to Poe were tackle Hector Cowen, guard Jesse Riggs, center William George and backfield men Roscoe Channing and Knowlton Ames. The Orange and Black once again went undefeated that year, winning all ten of their games and scoring 661 points to their opponents' 31.

From 1890 through 1893, the Old Nassau men were 46-4-1, winning the league with another undefeated record of 11 games in 1893. Philip King was the star, and he made All-America at quarterback in 1891 and 1893 and at halfback in 1892. In his four years of play, he scored 50 touchdowns and kicked 56 points-after. In his freshman year he scored 11 touchdowns in the Tigers' 85-0 rout of Columbia, and during his senior year he did most of the coaching. From 1891 to 1893 the Orange and Black shut out 31 of their 38 opponents.

The national champion Tigers of 1893 beat Cornell 46-0, Penn 4-0, Army 36-4 and Yale 6-0, the Yale victory breaking a 37-game Eli winning streak. Stars of the 1893 squad included King, Langdon 'Biffy' Lea and Arthur Wheeler. Lea played tackle from 1892 to 1895,

Top: *Philip King was a quarterback and halfback at Princeton from 1890-93, leading them to the national championship his senior year.*

Above: *Kicker Alex Moffat invented the spiral punt in 1881.*

Left: *A scene from the Princeton-Harvard game of 1889.*

four seasons in which Old Nassau compiled a 45-5-1 record, holding their opponents scoreless in 35 of those 47 games. Arthur Wheeler, a guard, made All-America in 1892, 1893 and 1894. Wheeler was the key force in a Tiger line which held 26 of 35 opponents scoreless and went 31-4-0 in those three seasons.

Johnny Poe was captain of the Tigers' team in 1895 and became the coach in 1896. At halftime during the Harvard game that year, he made a pep talk in which he coined the phrase 'A team that won't be beat can't be beat.' The Tigers went on to win the game. The star of Poe's 1896 team was the captain, Garrett 'Gary' Cochran. The team became famous as 'Cochran's Steamroller.' He made All-America in 1897, and it was said of him that 'he was a bull for strength and could stir his teammates to a frenzy.'

Another Poe – Arthur – a spectacular end who weighed only 150 pounds, was the hero of the Yale game in 1898. He stole the ball from Yale halfback Alfred Durston's hands, just as Durston was about to score, and ran 99 yards for a touchdown. The final score was Princeton 6, Yale 0.

A R T 'Doc' Hillebrand played from 1896 to 1899 on the Princeton team that won 43 out of 47 games, sharing the national championship with Harvard and the University of Michigan in 1898 and winning it outright in 1899. In those two years, the Tigers scored a total of 451 points to their opponents' 26. In 1898 they were 11-0-1, and in 1899 they went 12-1-0. Hillebrand came back to Princeton to coach from 1903 to 1905 and won 27 out of 31 games.

William 'Big Bill' Williams made All-America in 1899 when he was captain of the championship team that beat Yale for the second year in a row. In the 1899 edition, with the score 10-6 in favor of Yale and five minutes left to play, Princeton had the ball on the Yale 20 when Arthur Poe dropkicked a five-pointer to steal the game. He later said, 'It was the first dropkick that I had tried in my college career.'

Princeton's 1903 team, with Doc Hillebrand as coach, went through their first ten games undefeated, untied and unscored-on. The eleventh game, the last of the season, was against Yale, which was also unbeaten, having run up 290 points against 15 for their opponents. Yale jumped off to a 6-0 lead in the game. The Elis came right back again, heading down the field, but Princeton stopped them on the Tigers' 26-yard line. Ledyard Mitchell, the Yale placekicker, dropped back for a field goal attempt. The ball was snapped, and the left side of the Princeton line poured through toward Mitchell's kicking foot. John DeWitt, the Nassau guard, scooped up the ball and ran 70 yards for a touchdown. He also dropkicked the ball for the extra point to tie the score. With just a few seconds to go in the game, DeWitt got ready for another placekick from the Yale 53-yard line. He put all his weight into it, and the kick split the uprights. The final score was Princeton 11, Yale 6, and the Princeton Strong Boy had scored all the points. Princeton was the national champion, and had scored 259 points against their opponents' six.

Princeton fullback James McCormick made All-America twice and the All-American second team once from 1905 to 1907. The year he won the second team position was 1906, but the Tigers shared the league title with Yale that year, both with a 9-0-1 record. Both teams were awesome, Princeton outscoring its foes by 205-9, and Yale topping its opponents by 144-6. During McCormick's three years playing for Old Nassau, the Tigers won 24 games, lost only four and tied one. McCormick went on to coach Princeton in 1909, finishing with a record of 6-2-1. From 1908 to 1911, the Orange and Black went 26-5-6.

Princeton was back at the top in 1911, going 8-0-2 that year, winning the Ivy League and sharing the national championship with the University of Minnesota. Lehigh (6-6) and

Right: *Game action from the 1916 meeting of Princeton and Harvard in Ithaca, New York.*

Above: *William W Roper '02 coached at his alma mater for 17 years (1906-08, 1910-11 and 1919-30) and compiled a record of 89-28-16. His greatest year was 1922, when he fielded the undefeated Team of Destiny that beat the great Amos Alonzo Stagg's University of Chicago Maroons.*

Navy (0-0) were the only teams to tie the Orange and Black, which scored 179 points to its opponents' 15. Edward Hart was the captain of that team, and it wasn't until the season was over it was discovered that he had been playing with a fractured neck.

In 1911 Princeton finally beat Yale again, for the first time since 1903. They slipped by the Elis when end Sam White scooped up a Yale fumble from the wet turf and ran 50 yards for a touchdown to win the game, 6-3. The Tigers had another squeaker against Harvard, 8-6, when White grabbed a blocked kick and ran 95 yards across the goal line. Later in the game, White tackled Harry Gardner, who had just run back to retrieve a Tiger punt, and knocked him across the goal line for a safety to win the game. Princeton also beat Dartmouth, 3-0, on a single field goal.

Toward the end of the decade, a bright young man arrived at the Princeton campus eager to play football. He was only 5-feet 7-inches and weighed but 138 pounds, but when he learned that he was going to Princeton, he wired his mother in St Paul, Minnesota: 'Admitted. Send football pads and shoes immediately please. Wait trunk.' He showed up for practice and three days later was forced out for good with an ankle injury. But years later he was still sending suggested plays to the Tigers' coach. His name was F Scott Fitzgerald.

The 1919 Yale game was a strange one. Princeton center 'Whitey' Thomas got confused when he recovered a Yale fumble and headed toward his own goal line with the ball. He would have gone the whole route if halfback Maury Trimble had not felled him with a flying tackle. On the other hand, the Orange and Black won the game on a brilliant decision that was a perfect example of the Princeton football ethic of sacrifice for the cause. The score was

Above: *Princeton versus Yale at the Yale Bowl, 1908.*

tied, 6-6, with minutes to go. Yale had the ball at midfield and tried a lateral pass. The Eli receiver fumbled the ball, and Princeton's Hank Garrity was about to pick it up, but he realized that his teammate, Hank Sheerer, was a faster runner. Rather than pick up the ball, Garrity blocked a Yalie as Sheerer grabbed the pigskin and ran for the winning touchdown.

The 1919 Harvard game also featured a bonehead play, but this time it turned into disaster. Frank Murrey, a substitute, entered the game to replace a mediocre back, and announced to the referee, 'Murrey replacing Trimble.' Trimble was the star of the team, and he was not the player that Murrey had been sent in to replace. Because of this slip of the tongue, Trimble was forced to go to the bench, and Harvard tied the score with a last-minute pass into the area defensive zone formerly covered by Trimble.

William W Roper was the Princeton coach for 17 years, from 1906 to 1908, 1910 to 1911 and 1919 to 1930, and he was a master of locker room oratory. One of his players from the 1922 team said, 'Coach Roper was a true Princetonian from the old school. He convinced us that if we wore Orange and Black and the other side didn't, we had them licked.'

That 1922 group of players became the

'Team of Destiny.' Wingback Charley Caldwell, who would later become a Princeton coach himself, said, 'I guess we were surely that. We were strong defensively and won on Ken Smith's kicking and the breaks. Each Saturday the oddsmakers picked us on the short end, and we'd win, even though we lacked an attack. We had no blocking, no passing, no real ground game. Some of our plays were even made up in the huddle.' The Team of Destiny was really a so-so group, rolling up a

Top: *The 1922 Team of Destiny.*

Above: *Chicago's John Thomas (with ball) making the first touchdown of the Princeton-University of Chicago game in the first quarter on 28 October 1922. Princeton took home an amazing comeback victory, 21-18.*

mere 127 points in its eight games and allowing 34. But they simply refused to lose. Three of their triumphs were by a single field goal or a last-second touchdown. Yet they won, going undefeated, although Cornell beat them out for the Ivy League title because they, too, had gone undefeated and had won one more league game than the Tigers.

The highlight of the 1922 season was the game against the University of Chicago, and this was the first time that Princeton had gone to the Midwest. Just before the game, Chicago's bone-crushing steamroller was the 3-1 favorite. Both Chicago coach Amos Alonzo Stagg and Princeton coach Bill Roper later said that their 1922 clash was the most exciting game they ever coached. Going into the fourth quarter the Maroon was ahead, 18-7, and during that quarter Princeton was backed up to its own two-yard line. John Cleaves lined up in punt formation in his own end zone. He faked a kick, rolled to his right and passed to quarterback Johnny Gorman, who ran the ball to midfield. But Old Nassau could get no closer than the Chicago 42-yard line. This time Cleaves did punt, and Chicago was deep in its own territory. Then came a fumble and the ball bounced directly into the hands of Tiger end Howard Gray, who ran it in for a touchdown. After the conversion, the score was 18-14, with Chicago still ahead.

In the next series of plays, Princeton held the Maroon and got the ball back on their own 42.

They then proceeded to march the ball to the Chicago three. On fourth down, halfback Harry Crum hit the line, somehow wriggled free and fell into the end zone. Another conversion made the score 21-18. With two minutes to go, Chicago started passing and moved the ball to the Princeton six-yard line. Three plunges later the Maroon was on the Princeton one. Then, with seconds left, John Thomas got the ball and hit the line. In a spirited example of defense, Princeton held him on the two-foot line. The Orange and Black took over, punted, and the game ended with the Tigers the victors in a stunning upset.

At the end of the 1920s, Princeton suffered a downturn in its football fortunes. In Bill Roper's last two years as coach, 1929 and 1930, and Al Wittmer's single year at the helm, 1931, the Tigers' record was 4-16-2, and Old Nassau lost to Yale in all three of those years. Clearly something had to be done.

So Herbert O 'Fritz' Crisler was hired away from the University of Minnesota to coach the team for $8000 per year – the first non-alumnus coach in the history of the school. Since the beginnings of their rivalry, the Big Three schools (Princeton, Yale and Harvard) had stuck with a policy of having no coaches who had not graduated from the school and thereby come up through the ranks. But during the previous two years, the Tigers had won only one game a season, and in both games the victories were over their opening-day opponent – tiny

Above: *Herbert O 'Fritz' Crisler spent six seasons as coach at Princeton (1932-37). He led the Tigers to two Ivy titles (1933 and 1935).*

Below: *Yale punts during the 1933 Princeton-Yale game, which Princeton won. The Tigers went 9-0-0 for the season.*

Amherst College. In Crisler's first year, the Tigers went 2-2-3, at least an improvement, and they held Yale to a tie, 7-7. By 1933 Crisler had molded a winning team. The Orange and Black went undefeated in nine games, winning the Ivy title along the way. They scored 217

Above: *Dick Colman discusses a play with members of his fine 1957 team during his first season as coach.*

Far left: *Fullback Cosmo Iacavazzi helped bring the Ivy championship to Princeton in 1963.*

points to their opponents' eight, and would have gone to the Rose Bowl except for a Big Three agreement banning postseason games.

In 1934 Princeton lost only one of their eight games – to Yale, 7-0 – and scored 280 points to their foes' 38. Still, that one loss enabled Columbia to take the Ivy title, even though the Rose Bowl-bound Lions had been humiliated by Princeton, 20-0. In 1935 they went undefeated again in a nine-game schedule, winning the league championship by allowing only 32 points while scoring 322. Crisler once compared the 1933 and 1935 teams. 'The 1933 team was largely a sophomore group, and the striking thing about it was its defensive greatness. Since it is much easier to teach defensive football, it is understandable why sophomores were able to distinguish themselves. Starting with the defense as the basis, I began to build the offensive crew which culminated in the undefeated team of 1935.'

In the years that followed, things began to go downhill. Princeton went 4-2-2 in 1936 and 4-4 in 1937, and Crisler left to become one of the legendary coaches in the history of football at the University of Michigan. For the rest of the 1930s through the 1940s, the Tigers had a tough time. It wasn't until 1950 that they once again won the Ivy title. The only bright spot along the way was the tenure of Coach E E 'Tad' Wieman, from 1938 to 1942. His record was mediocre, a mere 20-18-3, but Princeton did beat Yale in four out the five games.

Charley Caldwell, one of the players on the 1922 'Team of Destiny,' returned to his alma mater in 1945 to become the coach who rebuilt

Opposite: *Action from the 1950 Dartmouth game, played at Palmer Stadium during Hurricane Flora. The Tigers beat the Big Green 13-7.*

Right: *All-America tailback Dick Kazmaier brought Princeton two straight undefeated seasons, 1950 and 1951. Probably the greatest all-around back in Princeton history, in three seasons he passed, ran and kicked for a total of over 4000 yards. He won the Heisman Trophy and the Maxwell Award in 1951.*

Above: *Charles W Caldwell played on the 1922 Team of Destiny and returned to his alma mater in 1945 as head coach. In 12 seasons (1945-56) Caldwell fielded two undefeated teams and two teams that won the Lambert Trophy, and brought the winning spirit back to Princeton.*

versity life, and the balance effected between the primary purposes of higher education and athletics, he is in for trouble.'

In 1949 a young halfback named Dick Kazmaier showed up for football practice. 'Kaz' was a frail-looking, pink-cheeked kid from Ohio, but by 1950 he was the star of the team, a superb runner who combined speed with remarkable changes of pace. He was also a great passer. In his three years on the team, he was to run for more than 4000 yards, score 20 touchdowns and pass for 35 more, although he stood only 5-feet 11-inches and weighed only 171 pounds.

The 1950 Princeton team was undefeated, going 9-0-0 and winning the Ivy title, beating Harvard 63-26 and Yale 47-12. *The New York Times* called them the finest Princeton eleven since 1935: 'In scoring its 12th successive victory since 1949, Princeton brought its point total for the season to 336. It thus excelled the modern Tiger record of 322 scored by Fritz Crisler's 1935 champions.'

In the Harvard game of 1950, Kazmaier scored four touchdowns in the first 11 minutes. In the Yale game, Kaz and Bill Kleinsasser drove for touchdowns of 50, 63 and 54 yards in a mere 12 plays. The season marked the fourth time in a row that Princeton had won the Big Three title. Needless to say, Kazmaier was on the All-America team.

The 1950 Dartmouth game was played during Hurricane Flora. Punting into the wind that day caused the ball to soar vertically and then blow backwards, often resulting in a loss of yardage. In a punt with the wind, the ball sometimes went 60 or 70 yards. There were only about 100 Princeton fans at the game in Palmer Stadium and but 10 or 12 Dartmouth supporters. Princeton fullback Jack Davidson later reported, 'There were pools of water an inch deep all over the field. The officials had to hold the ball and hand it to the center when he was ready to snap it. If they set it down it would float away.' Princeton won, 13-7, with Kaz running for both touchdowns.

In 1951 Caldwell had to rebuild. He had lost 25 of his 40 lettermen from the year before – ten of them first-string offensive players and six first-string defenders. Only Kazmaier remained in the backfield. They started out by blasting New York University, 54-20, then almost didn't win their second game. Navy battled them all the way before falling 24-20. Next they squeaked by Penn, 13-7. After that it was a breeze. The Tigers beat Lafayette 60-7, Cornell 53-15, Brown 12-0, Harvard 54-13, Yale 27-0 and Dartmouth 13-0, capping off a 22-game winning streak. Princeton ended the

the Princeton winning tradition. From October 1949 to November 1952, the Tigers had a streak of 30 wins in 31 games, and Caldwell was selected as Coach of the Year by the American Football Coaches Association in 1950 – the last Ivy League coach so honored. But he always understood the real function of a university. 'If a college coach doesn't understand just how the curriculum operates, what challenges his boys face in other phases of uni-

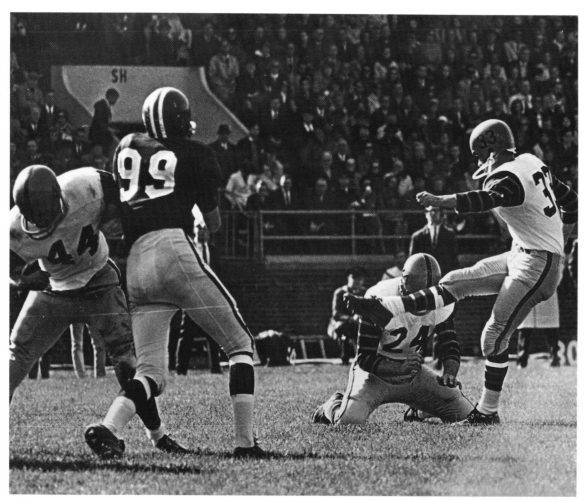

Left: *Placekicker Charlie Gogolak (33) contributed his toe to Princeton's efforts from 1963 to 1965.*

Below: *The 1966 'Cinderella' team that tied with Harvard and Dartmouth for the Ivy League title.*

Bottom: *Action from the 1969 Harvard game, where the Tigers quashed the Crimson 51-20.*

year by being ranked sixth in the country – the last Ivy school to be in the top ten. Not only did Kazmaier make the All-America squad, he was also awarded the Heisman Trophy as the best college football player in the country, beating out such luminaries as Babe Parilli of Kentucky, Johnny Bright of Drake and Hugh McElhenny of Washington. That year he had led the nation with a total offense of 1827 yards and in passing with a 62.6 percent completion rate.

Princeton challenged Yale for the Ivy title in 1955 by winning five of their last six games. The championship was riding on the Yale game, and the first half was scoreless, although Yale had outplayed the Tigers. Then, in the third quarter, Princeton recovered a fumble and turned it into a touchdown with Royce Flippen carrying the ball. The Tigers scored again later on an intercepted pass, and the final score was Princeton 13, Yale 0.

At the end of the 1956 season, Charlie Caldwell was stricken by cancer and turned over the reins to Dick Colman. On 1 November 1957, the day before the Dartmouth game, Caldwell died. In 1957 Colman had the finest group of sophomores as well as one of the strongest backfields in several years, centering around tailback Tom Morris and fullback Fred Tiley. Except for a 12-10 loss to Colgate,

the Tigers were 5-0 in the Ivy League going into the Yale game. Yale was 4-0-1, having been tied by Dartmouth. But Princeton was beaten in a 20-13 upset. Now everything hinged on the showdown between the Tigers and Dartmouth. Slogging through the snow and mud in Palmer Stadium, Princeton won the championship by defeating the Big Green handily, 34-14.

Princeton was not to win another championship until 1963, when they shared the crown with Dartmouth. In the opening game, fullback Cosmo Iacavazzi ran for 102 yards to beat Rutgers, 24-0. The next Saturday, it was Charlie Gogolak's soccer-style kicking that got the extra point for the Tigers in their 7-6 victory over Columbia. (On the same day, Charlie's brother, Pete, who also kicked soccer-style, kicked a field goal and three extra points as Cornell beat Lehigh, 24-0.) By the last game of the season, Princeton had a 5-1 record in the Ivy League, and all the Tigers had to do to clinch the title was defeat Dartmouth. That would prove to be easier said than done. Princeton built up a comfortable lead of 21-7 at the end of the third quarter, but Dartmouth was not to be denied, cutting the lead to 21-15. Then, with 5:35 left in the game, Iacavazzi fumbled on his own two-yard line, and Dartmouth's John McLean ran the ball in for a touchdown. The Indians won 22-21, and the two teams were co-champions. That year Iacavazzi tied with Dave Casinelli of Memphis State for the national scoring championship. Each had 84 points.

In 1964, Princeton had the title sewn up as it went into its final contest with a 6-0-0 record in the league. The final opponent was Cornell, with its 3-3-0 record. It was a wild battle, but the Tigers finally won, 17-12, capping off their first undefeated season since 1951. Oddly enough, the Tigers didn't win the Lambert Trophy as the best football team in the East – Penn State did.

The Tigers' next successful season was 1966, but they had to settle for a three-way tie in the Ivy League. Going into the last game of the season, Princeton, Harvard and Dartmouth were tied for first place with identical 5-1 Ivy League records. The Tigers beat Cornell, 7-0, the Crimson defeated Yale, 17-0 and the Big Green whomped Penn, 40-21, and the status quo remained.

In 1969 Princeton got off to a bad start, suffering a Rutgers drubbing (29-0) in a game marking the 100th anniversary of their first college football game. But they pulled themselves together, and five weeks into the season only Princeton, Dartmouth and Yale were

unbeaten in Ivy League play, and the Tigers had yielded only four first downs in their 42-0 blowout of Penn. Princeton went on to flatten Harvard, 51-20. The three leaders faltered at the end of the season, however, as Dartmouth beat Yale, Yale beat Princeton, and Princeton beat Dartmouth. The result was another three-way tie for the Ivy championship.

The 1970s started poorly for Princeton. They finished fifth in the league in 1970 (3-4 in the Ivies and 5-4 overall) and 1971 (3-4, tied with Yale, and 4-5). Things got worse in 1972, when they ended up tied for sixth with Columbia (2-4 and 3-5). But that was not the half of it. They fell to the cellar in 1973 (0-7 and 1-8). Then came three straight years of finishing fifth, 1974 (3-4, tied with Dartmouth, and 4-4-1), 1975 (3-4, 4-5) and 1976 (2-5, tied with Cornell, Pennsylvania and Columbia, and 2-7 overall).

Top: *Halfback Bobby Isom was a bright spot in an otherwise uninspired string of seasons in the mid-1970s.*

Above: *The team captains shake hands before the start of the 1969 Princeton-Dartmouth game.*

Above: *Action from the 1969 Rutgers-Princeton game celebrating the 100th anniversary of the first intercollegiate football game. Rutgers repeated their victory over the Tigers.*

In 1977, things were a little better as the Tigers climbed up to sixth place with a 3-4 record. The highlight of the season was undoubtedly the final game in which Princeton swamped Cornell, 34-0. Bobby Isom, the halfback, was the star, going 178 yards on 31 carries and scoring two touchdowns. But because of the Tigers' pitiful showing for the preceding few seasons, only 8667 people showed up in Palmer Stadium.

It was back to seventh place in 1978 with a 1-4-2 record, and Princeton barely edged Penn out for the cellar position as the Quakers turned in a 1-5-1 mark. In 1979 the men in Orange and Black had their first winning season since 1970, ending up 5-2 and 5-4. In the final game they beat Cornell, 26-14. In 1980 they were 4-3 and 6-4, good enough to tie Brown, Dartmouth and Harvard for third

place in the Ivy League. But they did it the hard way, beating Dartmouth in the final game, 27-24, after having to come from behind in the final quarter on two long passes from quarterback Mark Lockenmeyer to Chris Crissy and Lew Leone.

Princeton improved in 1981, finishing third with a 5-1-1 record in the league and a 5-4-1 overall mark. The thrill of the season was the final game triumph over Cornell, 37-14, with Larry Van Pelt closing out his career by scoring three touchdowns.

The Tigers finished with a 3-4 league record and 5-5 overall in the 1982 season, after being slaughtered in the final game by Dartmouth, 43-20. Things were worse in 1983, as Princeton was edged by Cornell, 32-30, in the final game and posted a 2-5 and 4-6 record. In 1984, Princeton's Derek Graham set an Ivy League

Above: *Larry Van Pelt contributed his running talents to the strong 1981 season, in which the Tigers went 5-1-1 in the league and 5-4-1 overall.*

Left: *Princeton's Chris Crissy (20) is knocked out of bounds by Harvard's Tom Masterson during second-quarter action in 1978.*

receiving record in the 21-17 win over Dartmouth. This victory ended a four-game losing streak and the Tigers finished with a 2-5 and 2-7 record.

Princeton fans had high hopes for the 1987 squad after a disappointing 1986 season in which they had an Ivy League record of 2-5 and an overall mark of 2-8. They were looking forward to seeing the three Garrett brothers play, sons of the former Columbia coach, Jim Garrett. Jason was to be the probable starting quarterback, Judd would be at halfback and John would probably be the backup split end behind flashy Jeff Baker.

Then tragedy struck. Coach Ron Rogerson died at the age of 44 on 8 August 1987. The cause was an apparent heart attack while jogging, and it happened just three weeks before fall football practice was to begin. Steve

Tosches was given the unenviable task of replacing him. Tosches had been the offensive coordinator for the Tigers and had previously coached for four years under Rogerson at the University of Maine. The first practice was a sad one, held after a memorial service for Rogerson.

The first game, on 19 September 1987, was a stunner. Despite all of Princeton's problems, they ran roughshod over Dartmouth, 34-3, with the Garretts running wild, combining for 342 yards. Jeff even caught two touchdown passes from Jason. They did it again the next week in a 42-6 victory over Davidson. Jason passed for 208 yards, Judd rushed for 101 yards and John caught four passes for 82 yards and a touchdown.

The Tigers lost to Brown in the last quarter, 13-7, but turned around and beat Columbia,

38-8, handing the Lions their 35th consecutive loss – a new futility record for major colleges. The following week was a triumph over Lehigh – a squeaker at 16-15. Princeton was beaten, 24-19, in the final two minutes by Harvard, the eventual Ivy champion. Then it was Penn's turn, and the Tigers triumphed, 17-7 – the first win over the Quakers since 1982. They were beaten by Colgate, 39-15, and Yale, 34-19, but the season ended with a happy 23-6 victory over Cornell, and the Tigers wound up with a better-than-expected 4-3 mark in the Ivy League and a 6-4 record overall. Loyal Princetonians remarked 'wait until next year,' and given their standout record in Ivy League play, no one doubted there would be a 'next' year for the Tigers of Princeton.

Top: *Record-setting receiver Derek Graham in action against Cornell.*

Above: *Coach Ron Rogerson.*

Above right: *Halfback Judd Garrett (40) who, with brothers Jason and John, would help bring the 1987 Tigers a 4-3 Ivy result and 6-4 overall.*

Right: *Quarterback Jason Garrett (17).*

Opposite top: *Placekicker Bob Goodwin (2).*

Opposite bottom: *Dean Cain (11) in 1987.*

YALE
UNIVERSITY

Founded: 1701
Location: New Haven, Connecticut
Undergraduate Enrollment: 5150
Colors: Yale Blue and White
Nickname: Bulldogs

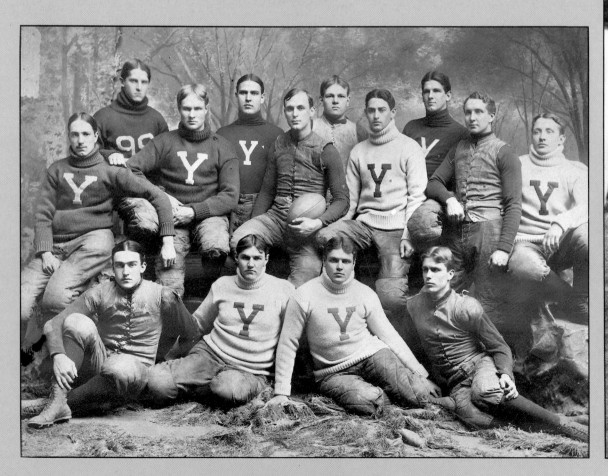

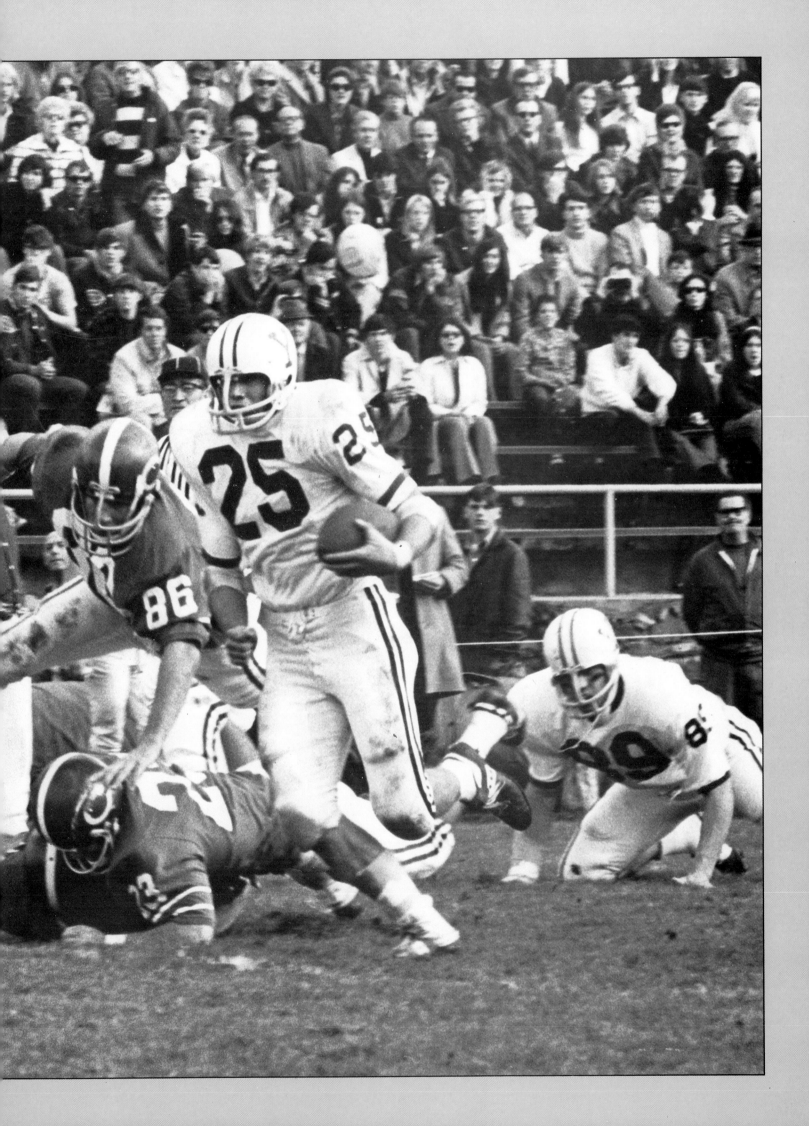

Be that as it may, football at Yale began with games between undergraduates, and in 1872 the Yale Football Association was formed to govern the sport. On 16 November of that year, 400 spectators watched Yale beat Columbia, 3-0, in its first intercollegiate game, at Hamilton Park in New Haven.

The next year, Princeton came up the coast by boat to New Haven, and Yale's supporters adopted the school's color, blue, to distinguish themselves from Princeton's orange. In 1875 Harvard challenged Yale to a game. At that time Yale still played a kicking game like soccer while Harvard played by rugby rules, so the two sides agreed to 'concessionary' rules, or a compromise. The teams met for the first

time on 13 November 1875, at Hamilton Park; 2000 people attended, even though the admission jumped from 25 to 50 cents. Harvard won 4-0, although over the decades Yale would pull well ahead in the series (which stands 56-40-8 for Yale through 1987).

Gene Baker, the captain of the 1876 Yale team, preferred rugby to soccer football, so he drilled his team on the running-tackling game. The year 1876 was also the first year Yale's team wore uniforms consisting of blue shirts with a big white Y, white trousers, blue stockings and blue caps. The year 1876 was also significant for the appearance on the Yale team of freshman Walter Camp. He would continue to play for Yale through 1882, as there was no three-year limit in those days, and was captain for three of those years. Although Camp was not a powerhouse player, his contributions to the rules and tactics of the game would make him the 'father of the game.'

Page 168: *The Yale football team of 1898.*

Page 169: *Agile tailback Dick Jauron (25) was a crucial element in the Yale offense from 1970-72. He still holds the Eli career record for rushing, with 2947 yards.*

Above: *Yale and other Ivy League schools in the late 1800s helped to popularize football as a sport suitable for fashionably-dressed spectators.*

Above right: *The Eli captain in 1876, Gene Baker, who preferred the running-tackling game that resembled rugby.*

Although Yale did not participate in the first officially recognized intercollegiate game of football, Yale tends to regard itself as the premier college football team of America. Part of this pride is undeniably based on the contributions of Walter Camp, the Yale player and coach who, as much as any single individual, reshaped what was essentially English rugby into American football. Part of the claim is also based on some impressive statistics: Throughout the decades, Yale has won more games (743 through 1987), scored more points (21,855) and produced more All-Americans (116) than any college in the nation.

Beyond their great seasons, rivalries and individual players, there are other reasons that college football seems almost synonymous with the Elis (so named after Elihu Yale, after whom the college was named) or the Bulldogs (so named after the college mascot). From Yale comes the song 'Boola Boola' that captures the spirit of the college game – and only Yale can boast that Cole Porter wrote a song ('Bulldog, Bulldog') expressly for its team. Yale even claims that tailgating originated around the Yale Bowl.

In 1878, Camp attended his first rules meeting with other East Coast colleges, and he attended every one until his death in 1925. His accomplishments include encouraging the other colleges to adopt 11-man teams; replacing the 'scrum' of rugby (in which a ball is tossed between two teams) with the 'scrimmage' (in which the center of one team conveys the ball to the quarterback); helping develop the use of 'downs,' initially set at five yards in three downs, to prevent a team from simply holding onto the ball to retain its lead or a tie; developing the calling of signals; and helping devise the modern system of varying points for a touchdown, field goal and safety. Camp's influence on the game is also evidenced by the 53 Yale men, Camp's pupils, who went on to become head football coaches at other colleges.

Yale had played without a special coach during the earliest years, but that didn't stop Yale teams from dominating the sport. In 1883, Yale had an 8-0 season, outscoring opponents 482-2, including a whitewash of Michigan, 64-0. In 1888, Walter Camp rejoined the Yale team as its coach, and he would stay through 1892, posting a 67-2-0 record. Camp's first year as coach was actually Yale's third consecutive unbeaten season, and arguably its best: The Blue outscored their opponents 698-0 in a 13-0 season. On the Yale team were All-Americans Amos Alonzo Stagg and William 'Pudge' Heffelfinger – virtual legends in American football – and freshman halfback 'Bum' McClung, who would score 500 points in his four season.

Yale had a 15-1 season in 1889 (the loss was to Princeton, 10-0) and a 13-1 season in 1890 (the loss this time to Harvard, 12-6). Then in 1891, Frank Hinkey appeared on the Yale scene. A four-time All-American, Hinkey's reckless, sometimes dangerous style resulted in only one lost game in his four years. His tackling was vicious, despite his 5-foot 7-inch, 147-pound frame.

Armed with Hinkey, Yale posted perfect 13-0 seasons in both 1891 and 1892. Yale fell to Princeton, 6-0, in 1893, but avenged that with a 24-0 win to cap a 16-0 run in 1894. Yale allowed only 13 points to their own 485 that year, with the 12-5 win over Army being the closest game. The Harvard game was so violent that a public uproar caused the series to be suspended until 1897.

Yale's 1900 team is regarded as many as the greatest in those first 28 years that Yale had been playing football. Captain Gordon Brown led the Bulldogs through a 12-0-0 season that included 10 shutouts, an 18-0 win over Army,

29-5 over Princeton and 28-0 over Harvard. Brown, an All-American guard, rivaled Heffelfinger as one of Yale's best linemen of all time.

From 1901 through 1906, Yale continued its winning ways, with Tom Shevlin, another All-American, the star player of those years. Then

Above: *The 1876 Elis (Walter Camp is second from left, top row).*

Top: *Burt L Standish's turn-of-the-century dime novels included adventures on the Yale gridiron.*

Left: *Considered the best team in early Yale football, the 1900 eleven, captained by linesman Gordon Brown (holding the ball).*

Bottom left: *In his four years as Yale's left end, Walter 'Pudge' Heffelfinger was the buttress of the unbeaten, untied teams of 1888 and 1891, which yielded no points to its opponents.*

Above: *Amos Alonzo Stagg played end on the unrivalled 1888 Yale team. He went on to coaching greatness at the University of Chicago.*

in 1907 Ted Coy made his first appearance on Yale's varsity, and during his three years he experienced only one loss – 4-0 to Harvard in 1908. In 1909, Coy captained one of Yale's greatest teams and probably its best defensive unit. The undefeated, untied and unscored-upon Bulldogs won the mythical national championship in 1909 with a lineup that included six All-Americans: Carrol Cooney, Ham Andrus, Henry Hobbs, Reed Kilpatrick, Steve Philbin, and Coy.

The glory of the 1909 season raised Yale's all-time record to an astounding 327-17, but it also signaled the end of the golden age when Yale had thoroughly dominated football. In the years 1910 to 1915, Eli teams compiled a 36-14-7 record, respectable anywhere except in New Haven: the 14 losses in the six-year span were more than Yale had suffered in the previous 34 autumns. In 1910, the year in which 15-minute quarters were introduced to football, Yale posted a 6-2-2, its worst record since 1875.

Two years later, when the touchdown was stabilized at six points and the field shortened from 110 to 100 yards, Yale's return to prominence was marked by a perfect record (7-0) entering Big Three play. But the Bulldog was tied at Princeton (6-6), then ran into a Percy Haughton-schooled group of talented Harvard sophomores who led a 20-0 shutout of Old Eli.

Yale would lose to Harvard in each of its next four contests, culminating in a 41-0 humiliation on 20 November 1915, in Cambridge. Coaching accounted for much of that; Haughton was Harvard's first professional coach, while Yale still used the outdated graduate coaching system installed by Camp. In

1913, against some resistance from Camp, Yale appointed its first professional coach, Howard Jones, who had coached Ted Coy's national championship team four years earlier. Jones didn't last long – only for the 5-2-3 season and the first loss to Harvard in Harvard Stadium, 15-5.

Frank Hinkey was then brought in on a three-year contract, but lasted only two. In 1914, he led Yale to a 28-0 win over Notre Dame that snapped the Irish's 27-game winning streak and showed that Yale could still play with the big boys. But the season went downhill from there with losses to Washington and Jefferson (13-7), Princeton (19-14) and Harvard (36-0). Yale collapsed to 4-5 the next year, the first losing season in Eli annals. Midway through the season, Hinkey's power was usurped and Tom Shevlin was brought in to help coach. Yale mastered a 13-7 upset of Princeton that year, but the next week Harvard trounced Yale, 41-0, and Hinkey was out.

In came T A D Jones, the quarterback of Yale's 1905-07 teams who had gone on to coach at Exeter. Jones would restore Yale to some of its former stature on the gridiron, as well as immortalize himself with his words to the Yale team: 'Gentlemen, you are about to play Harvard. Never again will you do anything as important.' Jones quickly led Yale to an 8-1 record in 1916 with a lineup that included four All-Americans: captain Clinton Black at guard; end George Mosely; tackle Artemus Gates; and halfback Harry Legore. The team demolished its first five opponents and won a sixth straight in closer fashion, 7-3 over Colgate, before Fritz Pollard of Brown ran wild for 184 yards in a 21-6 Bruin victory. But the Bulldogs regrouped to win the H-Y-P championship.

In 1917, play ceased because of World War I, though Yale fielded an unofficial team that won all of its three games against such opponents as Loomis Institute and New Haven Naval Base. There were no games in 1918, but the next year play resumed, albeit without the guidance of Jones, who was in government service for a year. Al Sharpe coached Yale to a 5-1 mark before the Eli blew its biggest two games to end the season – Princeton scored in the final minutes off a Yale fumble to win, 13-7, and Yale failed to score from the Harvard one-yard line and fell, 10-3.

Jones didn't fare much better upon his return. The 1920 season saw Yale shut out for the first time in Big Three play – a 20-0 loss to a powerful Princeton eleven and a 9-0 loss to Harvard. Under fire from Old Blues but supported by the graduate committee and his

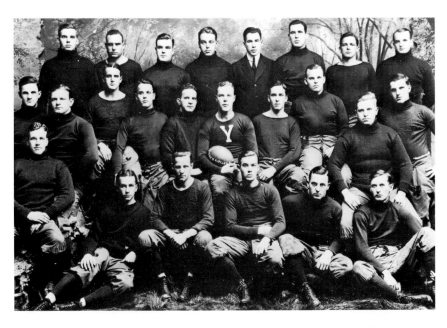

team, Jones was renewed to a three-year contract at $10,000 a year. This proved to be a good thing: Yale would lose only four games in the next four years and would post two unbeaten seasons.

Yale shut out its first four opponents in 1921 behind a sophomore nucleus of Ted Blair, Tony Hulman, Houston Landis, Jack Diller, Charlie O'Hearn and William Mallory. The Bulldogs entered the Harvard game with a perfect slate, 8-0, only to have a Harvard team that had lost to Princeton (whom Yale beat) two weeks earlier outplay Yale and win, 10-3.

After the previous season, the 6-3-1 mark in 1922 was considered a disappointment. Still, Yale lost by only 6-0 to an Iowa team that went on to win the Western Conference Championship, forerunner of the Big Ten. But Yale's real

Top: The 1909 team with captain Ted Coy (with ball), the last of Eli squads that thoroughly dominated early football.

Above: Coach T A D Jones (1916-27) led the first Eli win over a Percy Haughton Harvard team in 1916 and oversaw the illustrious teams of 1923 and 1924.

Left: Diminutive Yale end Frank Hinkey (1891-94) 'tackled like a fiend,' according to Princeton fullback Shep Homans '92.

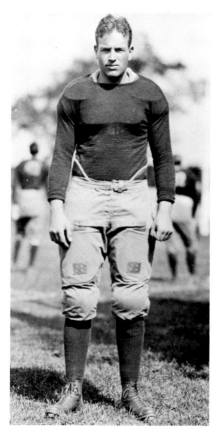

Above: *Walter Camp played halfback at Yale from 1876-82 and as his alma mater's coach from 1888-92, he distinguished himself as 'the father of football' by introducing rules that changed the game from rugby to modern football. Among other things he defined the scrimmage, the eleven-man team, signal calling and the QB position.*

Top right: *Winslow Lovejoy was captain and center for the strong 1924 Elis who finished 6-2-0.*

Above right: *R D Lumen was also a part of the impressive 1923 and 1924 Big Blue eleven.*

glory days were just around the corner.

In 1923, Yale fielded the Big Blue Team, which many consider the greatest team in Eli history. With two first-team All-Americans — fullback and team captain Bill Mallory, and tackle Century Milstead — and three second-team picks (Win Lovejoy, Lyle Richeson and Mal Stevens), Yale stormed to an 8-0-0 record, outscored its opponents 230-38, won the Big

Three title, the Championship of the East and a share of the National Championship. After hammering North Carolina, 53-0, and Georgia, 40-0, Yale upped its record to 5-0 with a 31-10 handling of Army before the largest crowd in Yale Bowl history, 80,000.

After blowing out the Tigers, 27-0, before 78,000 (the Bowl's third largest crowd of all time), the Eli entered a rainy and muddy Harvard Stadium determined to reverse the trend that had seen the Cantabs win eight of the last nine. Yale played like a champion, making few mistakes and capitalizing on Harvard's to prevail, 13-0, for the first time since T A D Jones' first Yale coaching year, 1916. That night in New York, 1000 Yale men marched over to the Harvard Club at 44th Street and sang: 'Good night, Poor Harvard/You're tucked in tight/ When the Big Blue Team gets after you/Harvard GOOD NIGHT!,' a song that now follows 'Bulldog' and 'Boola Boola' in the Yale Band's entrance medley before every game.

Yale didn't lose again in 1924, though Dartmouth (14-14) and Army (7-7) both tied the Eli. Yale won another Big Three crown by dumping Princeton, 10-0, and Harvard, 19-6, to go 6-0-2. Penn broke Yale's 18-game unbeaten streak on 17 October 1925, the same year that Walter Camp died. Yale would also lose to Princeton, 27-12, in a 5-2-1 campaign. Disaster struck the next fall when Yale, 3-0 to start, lost four consecutive games and was outscored in that stretch, 65-7. Jones announced that 1927 would be his last season at the helm.

Yale sent Jones out with a 7-1 record, the only blemish coming in a 14-10 loss to Georgia. He finished with a 65-18-4 career record. And even without All-American tailback Bruce Caldwell, who was ruled ineligible for the Princeton and Harvard games in his senior year because he had played as a freshman, Yale won the Big Three laurels with a 14-6 win over Princeton and a 14-0 triumph over Harvard in Cambridge.

In 1928, under new coach Mal Stevens ('25 of the Big Blue Team), Yale dropped its last three games to finish 4-4. Then in 1929 along came Little Boy Blue, the one and only Albie Booth, a New Haven native who captured the imagination of football fans across the nation. The 5-foot 7-inch, 144-pound Booth became affectionately known as The Mighty Mite. Though small, he could punt, placekick and pass, and his running was outstanding. In the 1929 Army game, Booth gained 233 yards from scrimmage in 33 carries, ran back a punt for 70 yards and scored all of Yale's points in a 21-13 win. It was hailed as the greatest single-game performance in Yale history.

Yale finished the 1929 season at 5-2-1, beating Princeton, 13-0, but losing to Harvard and Booth's rival, Barry Wood, 10-6. Another loss to Harvard in the 5-2-2 1930 season set up a final confrontation in 1931 between seniors Booth and Wood. Booth led Yale into Harvard territory, then kicked a field goal in the waning moments to give Albie his first win over the Harvards, 3-0. A week later, Yale closed its season at 5-1-2 with a 51-14 win over Princeton. Booth missed the finale due to pneumonia.

In 1932, Yale fell to 2-2-3, though Bob Lassiter's running provided a highlight in the 19-0 win over Harvard. Mal Stevens stepped down at season's end. The new coach, Reggie Root '26, lasted one year, the 4-4 season in 1933 when Yale lost to Harvard, 19-6, and to Princeton, 27-2. Raymond 'Ducky' Pond '25 became head coach in 1934, and a wisecracking sophomore end named Larry Kelley began his varsity career. Yale turned a mediocre 3-3 season into a memorable one with the Princeton game: Yale used the same 11 players without any substitutions throughout the entire game to stun heavily-favored Princeton, winners of 15 straight, 7-0. The next week, Yale shut out Harvard, 14-0, at the Bowl.

In 1935, the addition of Clint Frank, a fast, powerful runner in the mold of Ted Coy, gave Yale the outstanding one-two punch of Kelley and Frank. Yale beat Navy, 7-6, but lost to Army, 14-8, in successive weekends in October, and brought a 6-2 record into the finale with Princeton. But Fritz Crisler's best Tiger team walloped Yale, 38-7, with the only Eli touchdown coming on a 29-yard pass to Kelley.

In 1936, with Kelley as captain, Yale won seven of eight games. The only loss came to Dartmouth, 11-7, on 31 October at the Yale Bowl. In a 12-7 win over Navy, Kelley's kick of a fumble advanced the ball to the Middie 3 and Yale went in to score the winning touchdown. The controversial play caused a rule change: if a fumble is kicked, the ball is dead. Kelley scored in both of Yale's victories over Princeton (26-23) and Harvard (14-13), becoming the first Yale man ever to score in all six of his Big Three games. Kelley and Frank both were named first team All-America, and Kelley was named the second recipient of the Heisman Trophy.

Clint Frank led Yale to six victories in 1937 and a tie (against Dartmouth). A 26-0 handling of Princeton saw Frank run wild for 200 yards and four touchdowns. At Harvard Stadium, though, the Crimson prevailed, 13-6, with Frank hampered by a severely bruised knee. After the season, Frank, an All-American

Above: *Yale's halfback Albie Booth booted a drop kick for the deciding field goal, 3-0, in the 1931 50th anniversary game against Harvard, a fitting climax at the end of Booth's fine football career.*

Right: *Albie Booth, Yale's quintessential athlete, was captain of the football and basketball team and star of the baseball nine.*

for the second consecutive year, was named Yale's second consecutive Heisman Trophy recipient.

Yale suffered through its second losing season in history in 1938, though a narrow 15-13 loss to powerful Michigan on 22 October belied the play of a 2-6 team. After 3-4-1 and 1-7-0 marks in 1939 and 1940, Coach Pond departed and Spike Nelson took over, the first non-Yale man to coach the Bulldogs.

With the advent of World War II, Yale nevertheless decided to keep playing football, largely due to the feeling that Yale was the home of this American sport. In 1942, Howie Odell, an assistant coach at Wisconsin, came on as Yale's 28th head coach. In six years, Odell would lose just one Big Three game, a luxury not enjoyed by many other Big Three coaches (although it must be admitted that Harvard and Princeton didn't field teams every one of those war years).

College football got back on its regular track in 1946, when Yale compiled a 7-1-1 record. Its only loss was to Columbia, 28-20, despite an

Above: *Coach Jordan Olivar (1952-62) brought the 1956 Elis the first official Ivy League title with an 8-1 record.*

Right: *Larry Kelley, 1936 Eli captain, Heisman Trophy winner and sensational receiver.*

Top left: *Howie O'Dell left Wisconsin in 1942 to coach the Bulldogs from 1942 to 1948.*

Above: *Yale's Clint Frank in 1936. One of the finest all-around backs ever to play at Yale, he was an accurate passer, excellent blocker and speedy runner.*

84-yard kick return by freshman war veteran Levi Jackson. Odell's final season was a 6-3 year in 1947. In 1948, Herman Hickman, a rotund East Tennessean who was known for quoting long Victorian poems, arrived in New Haven after serving as Earl Blaik's line coach at Army. Yale posted a 4-5 mark that year, and Levi Jackson served as the first black captain in Yale's annals. The Yale line was so small that Hickman named them the Seven Dwarfs, but they were big enough to handle Harvard, 29-6, with Jackson scoring twice. Hickman lasted only through the 1951 season, due to his failure to control the Princeton and Harvard series.

The year 1952 is remembered by Yale football fans for two reasons: it began the era of coach Jordan Olivar, and it was the year that Yale allowed its manager, Charles Yeager, to suit up for the second half of the Harvard game and go in to catch a pass for the conversion point, adding to the 41-14 humiliation of Harvard. Ed Molloy and Denny McGill were two of the standout players during the next few years, but it was 1956 before Yale, with 30 of their 33 lettermen back, put it all together for an 8-1 season and the first official Ivy League title. Yale established new standards that year in yards rushing (2382), yards per game (264.7), per carry average (5.1), total offense (3199) and average gain (5.6). Denny McGill had a superlative season and finished with a record 21 touchdowns and a 7.1 yard-per-carry average, plus 1701 career yards rushing.

The next three years were 'building' ones for Coach Olivar and Yale's team, although there were some standout players – Dick Winterbaur, Herb Hallas, Tom Singleton and others – and a record-setting walloping of Harvard in 1957, 54-0. Then, in 1960, Yale put it all together to record its first undefeated, untied season in 37 years. Captained by Mike Pyle, the Bulldogs posted a 9-0-0 record, inevitably won the Ivy and Big Three titles, gained 14th place in the national standings, and took the Lambert Trophy.

Yet for all its glory, 1960 had a somewhat shaky start. Yale nearly lost the opener with UConn, when the Huskies drove to the Bulldog five with the score tied 8-8; Yale held them, and Wally Grant's 30-yard field goal provided the win. The next week, a struggling

Far left: *Yale's Dennis McGill was one of the notable players under Coach Jordan in the early 1950s.*

Above left: *Eli manager in 1952, Charles Yeager joined in the 41-14 trouncing of Harvard by catching a pass in the second quarter.*

Above: *Coach Carm Cozza has collected more victories than any other Eli coach.*

Left: *The program from the Yale-UConn game of 1963, with a drawing of Yale coach John Pont on the cover. His short coaching tenure covered the years 1963 to 1964.*

Brown team played stubborn, and Yale won by only 9-0. Yale then went on a roll that couldn't be stopped. Against Columbia, Kenny Wolfe broke open a tie with an 87-yard kick return. Against Colgate, Bob Blanchard threw a 37-yard touchdown pass and returned an interception for 99 yards. Yale held formidable Dartmouth to 60 yards rushing, and Penn to 39. Against Princeton, Yale followed its season-long pattern by jumping out to a big lead, going into the fourth quarter 36-6, behind three touchdown passes by Tom Singleton. Kenny Wolfe caught two of these. Against Harvard, Yale settled things early when Wolfe broke away on a 40-yard touchdown run on the first play in a 39-6 game.

In 1961 and 1962, however, Yale collapsed to 4-5 and 2-5-2 seasons respectively, and Olivar retired at the end of 1962 with a 61-32-6 record. For the next two years, Yale was coached by John Pont, who came from Miami University of Ohio with an entirely new staff. The two years under Pont had their ups and downs, but the biggest disappointment came at the end of the 1964 season, when Yale had a 6-0-1 record going into Big Three play. An injury to star runner Chuck Mercein in the Princeton game deflated Yale, who fell to the Tigers, 35-14, and then to Harvard, 18-14. Mercein's career, though cut short, brought him within 60 yards of Levi Jackson's rushing record (2049 yards).

Pont resigned at the end of the season to become head coach at Indiana, and eight days later one of his assistants, Carmen Cozza, was

OFFICIAL PROGRAM YALE·UCONN

SEPTEMBER 28 1963 FIFTY CENTS

introduced as his replacement. A young head coach at 34, Carmen Cozza has stayed on at least into 1988 to become an institution at Yale, having become the winningest coach in Yale history (139-70-4) and the winningest active Ivy League coach. But his debut was one that he and Yale would rather forget: Yale fell to UConn, 13-6, the first loss ever to its intrastate rival.

In 1966, however, there was great anticipation as Yale added two nationally recruited athletes to its varsity roster – Brian Dowling

Left and below: *Yale halfback Calvin Hill (30) exhibited the sprinting-receiving capabilities in college and pro performance which merited him Rookie-of-the-Year honors on the NFL's Dallas Cowboys in 1969.*

and Calvin Hill. But Dowling injured his knee in a rainstorm game against Rutgers, only the second game of the season, and was out for the rest of it. His replacement, Pete Doherty, ended up setting several records during the season, but Yale finished with only a 4-5 record after losing to both Princeton and Harvard.

Dowling had an injured wrist even before the 1967 season began and had to sit and watch as Yale dropped its opener to Holy Cross, 26-14. The Bulldogs, however, would not lose again until 1 November 1969. By the third game of 1967, Dowling was able to come in for one play, and there was no stopping Yale. The Bulldogs defeated Dartmouth, 56-15, and Princeton, 29-7. But it was against Harvard that the 1967 Bulldogs really came through. Favored Yale went up 17-0 in the second quarter, thanks partly to Dowling's scrambling abilities and a 40-yard touchdown pass to Hill. But Harvard scored just before halftime and immediately in the second half to cut the margin to 17-13. With only three minutes left, Harvard went ahead 20-17; Dowling responded with a 68-yard touchdown pass and a 24-20 lead. Harvard then drove down to Yale's 10-yard line, but Pat Madden recovered a Crimson fumble to preserve Yale's Ivy League championship, its first since the undefeated 1960 season.

The 1968 season turned out to be even more exciting, as seniors Dowling and Hill proved an unstoppable combo. (Hill would go on to collect rookie-of-the-year honors in the NFL as a Dallas Cowboy.) And the ultimate showdown came about when for the first time in 60 years, both Harvard and Yale entered The

Game undefeated. Both brought 8-0 records into Harvard Stadium, but Yale was given the edge because of its dominating style – Harvard had won its games in closer fashion. Yale went out to a 22-0 lead but just as in their 1967 meeting, Harvard scored before the half and again in the third period to cut it to 22-13. Yale then seemed to take control as Dowling scored from the five with only 10 minutes left and a 29-13 score. Yale was about to add to its lead before fumbling at the Harvard 14 with 3:34 remaining. By a series of plays, penalties and miracles that are best recounted as Harvard lore, the Crimson ended up with a 29-29 'win.'

The departure of Dowling and Hill looked ominous for 1969, and sure enough, Yale lost to UConn, 19-15, only the second loss ever to this rival. Then on 1 November, Yale lost to

Opposite: *From 1966 to 1968 the talents of QB Brian Dowling (10) dynamically complemented those of halfback Calvin Hill. For example, in the 1967 Harvard game Dowling completed a 40-yard TD and then a 68-yard TD, both to Hill.*

Dartmouth, 42-21, the Bulldogs' first loss in 18 Ivy League games over three seasons. But Yale rebounded and ended up with the Big Three crown, sharing the Ivy League title with Dartmouth and Princeton.

Yale finished out of the top spot the next four autumns, with three second places and an uncharacteristic fifth in 1971. A speedy tailback named Dick Jauron dominated the Yale offense from 1970 to 1972, rushing for 962 yards as a sophomore and becoming the first 1000-yard single-season rusher in Yale history, with 1055 yards in 1972. Jauron finished his Yale career as the Elis' all-time rusher with 2947 yards, a record that still stands.

In 1972, Yale celebrated its 100th year of intercollegiate football with a black tie dinner at the Waldorf Astoria, and Jauron got the landmark season off to a record-breaking start when he ran for 194 yards, a best single game showing, to spark a 28-7 win over UConn. Sophomore quarterback Tom Doyle rushed for 160 yards and one 64-yard run in Yale's 45-14 win over Dartmouth. But losses to Cornell and Penn left Yale a half game behind Dartmouth in the contest for the Ivy League crown, although Jauron won the Bushnell Trophy as the Ivy League Player of the Year.

In 1973, Yale went into The Game with a 5-3 record against favored Harvard (7-1), but

Top: *Bulldog John Rogan (19) attempting a pass in a game versus Navy in 1980.*

Above: *John Pagliaro endeavoring to dodge the Crimson in 1977.*

Left: *Tête-a-tête between John Pagliaro and Coach Cozza during The Game in 1976.*

Kevin Rogan, a reserve quarterback, led an upset win, 35-0. In 1974, Harvard got its revenge. The Bulldogs swept through their first six Ivy League games undefeated and untied and came into Harvard Stadium, just as in 1968, with an 8-0-0 record. Harvard scored with 15 seconds to go and defeated Yale 21-16, despite Gary Fencik (of recent Chicago Bears fame) who set Yale receiving records with 11 catches for 187 yards.

Yale's 10-7 loss to Harvard in 1975 dropped the Elis to third place behind Harvard and Brown in their league. But a 24-14 win over Penn on 8 November lifted Carmen Cozza to all-but-legendary heights as Yale's winningest coach with 68 victories, one more than the immortal Walter Camp. After the 1976 season, it was announced that Cozza would move on to become Yale's Director of Athletics, but after a short time, Cozza changed his mind: 'I am first, and above all else, a football coach.'

The Elis came through for Cozza in 1977, winning their second consecutive Ivy and Big Three crowns. Star of this as of the 1976 season was John Pagliaro, a New Haven boy, who had especially memorable moments in his two final games, against Princeton and Harvard. In the Harvard game, though, the biggest play

Above: *Curt Grieve (shown here) and John Rogan were record-setting passing partners. One of Coach Cozza's most satisfying memories was Rogan's 25-yard TD pass to Grieve in Navy's end zone for a spectacular 23-19 finale.*

Left: *A top middle guard in the nation, Kevin Czinger (40) zaps UConn QB Ken Sweitzer in 1981.*

Above: *Yalie QB Phil Manley (5) in 1980, supported by the Yale bulwark.*

was carried out by Yale punter Mike Sullivan, who adlibbed a fake punt and ran for a 66-yard touchdown in the fourth quarter to put Yale in command. Pagliaro won the Bushnell Trophy in both 1976 and 1977.

The 1978 season ended up at 5-2-2, but Yale set out after the Ivy League championship again in 1979, sparked by the defensive play of Tim Tumpane (eventual Ivy League Player of the Year) and Kevin Czinger, an irrepressible, if small, middle guard from Cozza's hometown of Parma, Ohio. But it was a sophomore

quarterback, John Rogan, whose 12-yard pass to Bob Rostomily gave Yale a 23-20 win over Cornell in Ithaca on 6 November and made Yale the first college in the nation to gain 700 football victories. After disposing of Princeton, 35-10, Yale – already having clinched the Ivy title – appeared certain to finish unbeaten and untied for the first time in 19 years. But 72,000 at the Yale Bowl saw the underdog Crimson (only 2-6) win, 22-7.

The 1980 season saw Yale end up with an 8-2 record, including a 17-16 win against the

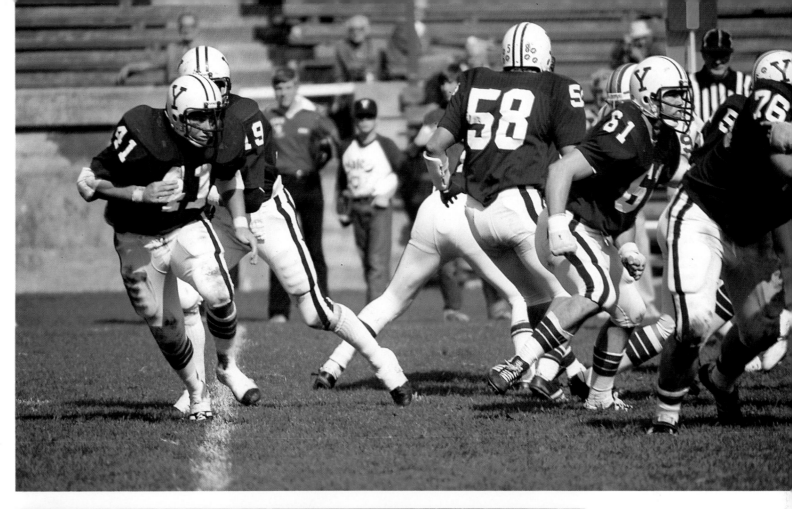

Above: *Yale captain and fullback John Nitti (41), Class of '80.*

Left: *Tailback Rich Diana (33), an All-Ivy electee, in the 1981 contest against Navy.*

Air Force and a 27-9 loss to Boston College (in Yale's first night game.) Against the Ivy League, Yale was 6-1, the loss being an upset by Cornell. Yale went into The Game with both teams at 7-2 overall and 5-1 in league play. But the Bulldogs, who would finish the season second only to Pittsburgh in rushing defense and ninth in overall defense, held the Crimson's rushing attack to -11 yards. Curt Grieve's leading catch from John Rogan in the open end of Harvard Stadium was all Yale needed, but Captain John Nitti closed out his career with a one-yard touchdown. Yale's defense was spearheaded by Kevin Czinger, named New England and Ivy League Player of the Year. The 1980 season also marked the emergence of Rich Diana, a junior tailback who ran with the power of a fullback. Diana, a first-team All-Ivy selection, went over the 100-yard mark five times in 1980 for a total of 1074 yards.

In the 1981 season opener against Brown, Diana shattered the Yale single-game rushing mark with a 196-yard day that gave the Bulldogs a 28-7 win. Yale's 1981 team also included the record-setting passing combination of John Rogan and Curt Grieve, and a defense that featured six All-Ivy (three first-team) players and future Dallas Cowboy Jeff Rohrer. When Navy came to New Haven in the third week of the season after its 21-16 loss to Michigan, 38,000 Yale Bowl fans and an ABC regional TV audience would see how good this Yale team was. The Midshipmen jumped out to a 12-0 first-quarter lead, but Yale then rallied. The biggest moment of Rogan's big day (16 of 30, 202 yards, three touchdowns) came near the end, when he found Grieve in the end zone for a 25-yard touchdown that gave Yale the win, 23-19. Cozza called it the biggest win out of the league in his career.

Yale needed more last-second heroics in a showdown of New England powers against

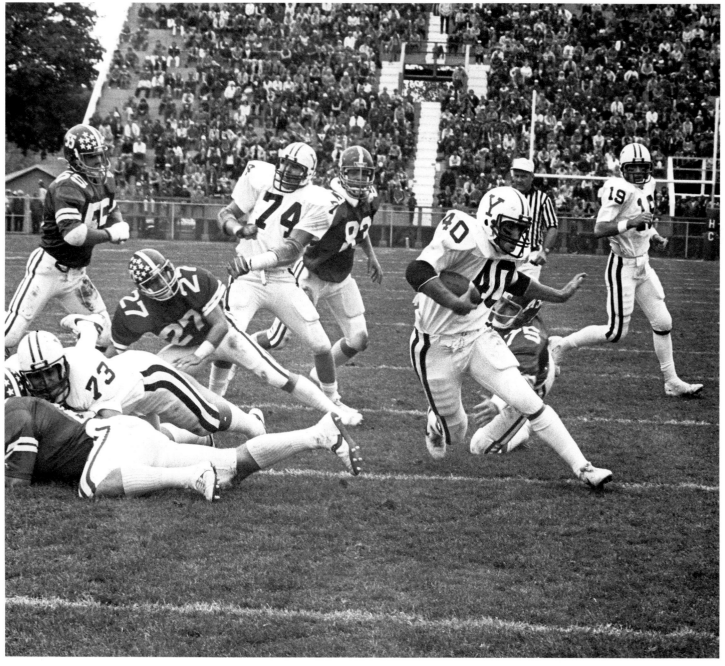

Opposite top: An ABC network television audience and 38,000 Yale Bowl spectators witnessed the Elis take command over the Midshipmen in 1981.

Opposite bottom: Eli Paul Andrie (40) rushing in 1983 against Holy Cross. Yale fans were disappointed by a 1-9 record that year, the worst in over a century.

Above: A first quarter play in the October 1981 Navy game, which did nothing to sway Navy's 12-0 lead. Yale soon thereafter rallied to a 23-19 victory.

Holy Cross the very next week: With 35 seconds left, Tony Jones kicked a 32-yard field goal to give Yale a 29-28 win. When Yale took on a 3-5 Princeton team, Yale looked unbeatable: It had an 8-0-0 record going, not to mention 14 straight wins over Princeton. The Eli jumped out to a 21-0 lead, made it 31-22 in the fourth quarter (after Princeton briefly took a 22-21 lead), and controlled the ball for 38:19 of the game, chiefly behind Diana's record 222-yard performance. But with only four seconds on the clock, Tiger quarterback Bob Holly bootlegged it in for a 35-31 upset. Stunned, Yale regrouped the next week to cap a 9-1 season with its second consecutive shutout of Harvard, 28-0, played in the Yale Bowl before 75,300, the largest crowd to witness such an event in New England since 1924.

A year later, things changed considerably. Yale, like the other Ivies, was made part of Division 1-AA, a demotion most Yale alumni resented since so much of football was rooted in Yale (and Yale qualified in stadium size and average attendance for 1-A status). On the field, it was not much better. The team suffered its first losing season in 11 years with a 4-6

mark, as the Bulldogs' three-year Ivy reign gave way to a new force, Penn, despite Joe Dufek's 232-yard passing in a 27-14 loss at Franklin Field. Yale did manage to beat Princeton, 37-19, but Harvard made up for its two-year scoring drought in The Game by walloping Yale, 45-7.

Yale's fortunes bottomed out in 1983 when the Eli lost nine of ten games, the worst season on the books in 111 years. The lone win came at Princeton, where Yale had brought its 8-0 record two years before and suffered a loss; this time the Bulldogs left with a 28-21 upset, thanks mainly to Paul Andrie's 167 yards rushing. The much-awaited (and hyped) 100th meeting of Yale and Harvard proved anticlimactic to the 70,097 fans, who had paid a record $20 apiece for tickets, because of Yale's obvious weakness, but Harvard first had to break a tie to win, 16-7. As the season worsened, there was discord in the Yale camp and speculation in the press as it was rumored that the Yale administration was pulling the rug on the football program.

Much of the controversy was forgotten by the end of the 1984 season, when Yale

Above: *Harvard's Pat Coyne (17) seizing Eli Bob Keenan (81) in 1984. After lagging 14-0 and then 27-20, Yale surged forward to a tense 30-27 win.*

Right: *In this scene from the Centennial Game, Yale tied Harvard 7-7. However, any hope of reversing Yale's misfortunes of 1983 died when the Crimson broke the tie to win 16-7.*

rebounded to finish 6-3. In some of the highest drama ever witnessed at the Bowl, for instance, Yale was trailing Princeton in the fourth quarter, 24-20; the Bulldogs held Princeton on a fourth and goal (on the two), then went 98 yards in the game's final 1:31 without using a time out to score on a pass from Mike Curtin to Kevin Moriarty. With five seconds left, Yale had won, 27-24. And after falling behind 14-0 and 27-20 against Harvard, Yale made it back one more time in a dramatic 30-27 win on Ted Macauley's fourth-down leap at the goal line for the winning touchdown.

The return of Curtin and Moriarty, along with the heralded sophomore quarterback Kelly Ryan, was cause for anticipation in 1985.

But Yale never really found its rhythm in that 4-4-1 year. This was the year that Yale suffered the worst defeat in its entire history, a 59-16 loss to West Point. But the Bulldogs regrouped for the final game and managed to knock the Crimson out of first place in a surprisingly easy win, 17-6.

Injuries to the top three quarterbacks by the first game of the season more or less doomed the 1986 campaign, which ended 1-7. Kelly Ryan went down the week before the opener but returned to rewrite records with his 426 yards passing (29 of 48) against Army, which won 41-24.

In 1987, Ryan lived up to billing in a spectacular senior campaign, leading Yale to a 7-3

Opposite: *Jeff Cramtton (87) tries to abscond with the ball in spite of Cornell opposition in 1984. Yale bounced back to a respectable 6-3 season.*

record that featured last-minute wins and some of the best offensive totals since the Dowling days. The season also featured a first as Yale traveled to Honolulu to take on the University of Hawaii on 3 October. The 62-10 Hawaii victory suggested Yale was playing out of its league. After dropping an error-filled opener to Brown, 17-7, Yale won three straight games with 30 seconds or less remaining – against UConn, William and Mary, and Penn. Yale then beat Cornell, 28-9, behind 252 yards passing by Ryan. Yale's best outing of 1987 came the next week when it beat Princeton, 34-19, for the 18th win over the Tigers in the past 20 contests. Ryan's 20 for 31, 329 yards, and three touchdowns for the day put him over the 4000-yard mark in his career. Tight end Dean Athanasia, already Yale's all-time best receiver, hit the 100 career reception mark with his seven-catch, 159-yard, two-touchdown afternoon.

The win over Princeton set up a winner-take-all showdown for the Ivy League title, as Yale and Harvard brought identical 7-2 overall and 5-1 league marks into The Game. On a day many will long remember for its −19° wind-chill-factor weather, Harvard prevailed, 14-10, before 66,548 diehard fans. Yale's miracle season nearly finished on cue when the

Eli drove into Harvard territory with less than two minutes to go, but the Crimson recovered a fumble at the 34 and held on to take the Ivy League title.

Kelly Ryan finished his career with 11 different Yale passing records and gave Yale its first Ivy League Player of the Year since Rich Diana. It was a reminder, if such was needed, of Yale's glorious history as a football power, and a sign that the glory days were far from over.

Top: *QB Kelly Ryan (6) crusaded the Elis to a 7-3 1987 season. Ryan holds 11 Yale passing records.*

Above: *With five seconds left, Kevin Moriarty nabs a pass from Mike Curtin to snatch the victory from Princeton, 27-24.*

Ivy League Football Champions (since league formalized in 1956)

Year	School	Year	School	Year	School	Year	School
1956	Yale (7-0)	1966	Dartmouth (6-1)	1972	Dartmouth (5-1-1)	1981	Dartmouth (6-1)
1957	Princeton (6-1)		Harvard (6-1)	1973	Dartmouth (6-1)		Yale (6-1)
1958	Dartmouth (6-1)		Princeton (6-1)	1974	Harvard (6-1)	1982	Dartmouth (5-2)
1959	Pennsylvania (6-1)	1967	Yale (7-0)		Yale (6-1)		Harvard (5-2)
1960	Yale (7-0)	1968	Harvard (6-0-1)	1975	Harvard (6-1)		Pennsylvania (5-2)
1961	Columbia (6-1)		Yale (6-0-1)	1976	Brown (6-1)	1983	Harvard (5-1-1)
	Harvard (6-1)	1969	Dartmouth (6-1)		Yale (6-1)		Pennsylvania (5-1-1)
1962	Dartmouth (7-0)		Princeton (6-1)	1977	Yale (6-1)	1984	Pennsylvania (7-0)
1963	Dartmouth (5-2)		Yale (6-1)	1978	Dartmouth (6-1)	1985	Pennsylvania (6-1)
	Princeton (5-2)	1970	Dartmouth (7-0)	1979	Yale (6-1)	1986	Pennsylvania (7-0)
1964	Princeton (7-0)	1971	Cornell (6-1)	1980	Yale (6-1)	1987	Harvard (7-0)
1965	Dartmouth (7-0)		Dartmouth (6-1)				

Overall Records of Ivy League Football Teams: 1869-1987

Team	Year Started	All Games GP	W	L	T	vs Ivy Teams GP	W	L	T
Yale	1872	1032	743	225	54	547	340	174	33
Princeton	1869	984	666	270	48	517	298	195	24
Harvard	1874	1013	679	285	49	518	283	209	26
Dartmouth	1881	900	552	305	43	478	252	205	21
Pennsylvania	1876	1085	659	384	42	464	230	220	14
Cornell	1887	899	514	362	33	451	190	245	16
Brown	1878	930	466	425	39	441	140	286	15
Columbia	1870	799	303	455	41	421	103	307	11

(Numerals in *italics* indicate illustrations)

Aberthaw Construction Company, Boston 102
Adams, Caswell 6
Alabama, University of 16
All-Americans 16, 17, 18, *20*, 27, 40, *50*, 50, 60, 64, *65*, 65, *70*, 72, 76, 81, 83, 87, 89, 89, 94, 100, *102*, 104, 106, *107*, 132, *133*, 134, 136, *140*, 142, 155, 156, *156*, 161, 162, 171, 172, 173, 174, 175
Allard, Don 125
American Broadcasting Company (ABC-TV) 121, 184, *185*
Ames, Knowlton 155
Amherst College 11, 16, 21, 81, 82, 110, 160
Anderson, John 29, 30, 31, 32, 36
Andrews, Benjamin 16
Andrews, Buff *20*
Andrews Field *16*, 17, *19*
Andrews, Harold 'Buzz' 18
Andrie, Paul 185, *185*
Andrus, Ham 172
Antonellis, Joe 123
Army (U.S. Military Academy) 47, 48, 49, *50*, 50, 68, 69, 104, 106, 108, *139*, 139, 155, 171, 174, 176
Asack, Bob 50
Athanasia, Dean 188
Atwell, Larry 25
Auburn University 72
Aug, Tom *74*, 76
Avila, Phil *13*

Backus, Ed *120*
Bad Hand, Howard 81
Baker Field 40, 49
Baker, Gene 170, *170*
Baker, Jeff 165
Baker, Whit 67
Balish, Christopher *98*
Barabas, Al 46, *47*
Barrett, Charley *47*, 62
Bateman, Bob 30
Baughan, Maxie *10*, 76, *76*
Beard, Mickey 92
Beatrice, Pete *29*, 30, 32, 36
Bednarik, Chuck 139, *140*, 142
Bell, Alex 110
Bell, Jim *129*
Bellizeare, Adolph 'Beep Beep' *142*, *143*, 144
Bergstrom, Brian *10*
Berlinger, Barney *140*
Berndt, Jerry 125, 145
Bigby, Kieron *34*, 36
Big Green *See* Dartmouth College.
Big Red *See* Cornell University.
Bingham, Bill 106-7
Biondi, Larry *52*
Bishop, Morris 59
Bissinger, Mike *52*
Black, Clinton 173
Black, Lee 50
black players 107, 176
Blackman, Bob *70*, 72, *72*, 76, *88*, 89, 91, 92, *93*, 93, 94
Blaik, Earl Henry 'Red' 49, 50, 68, *87*, 87, 88, 89, *89*, 176
Blair, Ted 173
Blanchard, Bob 177

Blitz, Jerome 'Jerry' *108*, 108
Bohrman, Swifty 67
Booth, Albie 87, *104*, 104-5, 174, *175*, 175
Booth, Ken 105
Boston College 65, 83, 94, 183
Botsford, Matt 108
Boulris, Chet 110-11
Bowden, Murray *93*, 93
Boyd, W N *152*
Bradlee, Fred *102*
Brewer, Charles 100
Brickley, Charlie *102*, 103
Bright, Johnny 162
Broda, Hal 21, *22*
Brooke, George H 132, *133*, 134
Brooks, William 100
Brown, Gordon 171, *172*
Brown, Larry *117*, *118*, 123
Brown, Ron 32
Brown Stadium 21, 22, *31*, 32, *37*
Brown University 6, 6, 10, 11, 16-37, *37*, *48*, 52, *54*, 71, 72, *75*, 76, *81*, 81, 84, 87, 91, 94, 97, 108, 110, *111*, 111, 115, 118, 120, 121, 125, 129, 134, 136, 139, 142, *146*, 148, 164, 173, 177, 181, 188, 189
Bruins *See* Brown University.
Bruni, Jim 145, 148
Buckeyes *See* Ohio State University.
Bucknell University 76, 115, 128, 145, 148
Bulldogs *See* Yale University.
Burr, 'Hooks' 103
Bushnell Cup 145, 148, 180, 182
Busik, Bill 106
Butler, Doug *152*
Butler, John 18, *20*
Butts, Al 52, *54*

Cadets *See* Army.
Cain, Dean 166
Calder, Charles 83
Caldwell, Bruce 174
Caldwell, Charlie 158, 160, 161, *161*, 162
Callinan, Jim 123, 125, *125*
Camp, Walter 8, 11, 17, 18, *20*, 40, *59*, 62, 81, 82, 100, 103, 134, 136, 153, 154, 170, *170*, 171, 172, 173, *174*, 174, 181
Campbell, Bill 50
Campbell, David 102
Canadian Football League 32, 118
Cannell, Jackson 83, *83*, 87
Carbone, Larry 32, *32*, 36
Carlisle Indians *20*, 102
Caron, Roger *123*
Casey, Eddie 103, 104
Casinelli, Dave 163
Cassidy, Charley *62*, 62
Cataldo, Walt 37
Cavanaugh, Frank 82, *83*, 83
Champi, Frank *115*, 116, 118
Chandler, Scott 148
Channing, Roscoe 155
Chapa, Ruben *30*, 32
Chasey, Jim 92, *93*, 93
Cheek, Marion *105*
Chicago Bears 48, *48*, 121, 181
Chicago, University of 85, 136, 139, *157*, 158, *158*, 172
Chiofaro, Don *113*, 113
Chollet, Hillary 69

Choquette, Paul 27
Church, Fred 104
Clark, Danny 37
Clasby, Dick 108
Cleaves, John 159
Cleveland Browns 27, 52
Cochran, Garrett 'Gary' 156, *156*
Cohane, Tim 106
Coleman, Dennis *29*, 30
Colgate University 22, 27, 29, *59*, 60, 62, 67, 68, 69, 81, 162, 166, 173, 177
Colman, Dick *160*, 162
Colo, Don 27
Columbia Broadcasting System (CBS-TV) 40
Columbia University 6, 8, 11, 25, 27, 29, 30, 32, *38*, 40-55, *55*, *59*, 68, 70, 71, 76, 87, *90*, 91, 93, 94, 111, 113, 115, *120*, 128, 134, 139, 142, 144, *147*, 148, 153, 155, 160, 163, 165, 170, 177
Comizio, Rich 145
Connecticut, University of 176, 177, *177*, 180, *181*
Conroy, Bob 41
Considine, Charlie 21, *22*
Conway, Pat 115
Cool, Gib 62
Coolidge, Jeff *102*
Cooney, Carrol 172
Cornell University 10, *10*, *13*, 29, 30, 36, 37, 40, *48*, 52, *58*, *59*, 59-76, 83, 84, *85*, 87, 89, 91, *91*, 93, 94, *95*, *111*, 111, *113*, 115, 125, 128, *132*, 132, 134, 136, *138*, 139, *140*, 142, 144, 145, 148, 153, 155, 159, 161, 163, 164, 166, 182, 183, *186*, 188, 189
Cornsweet, Al 21, *22*
Cougars *See* Washington State.
Council of Ivy Group Presidents 8
Courtier, Sanford 89
Cowen, Hector 155
Coy, Ted 172, *173*, 173, 175
Coyne, Pat *186*
Cozza, Carmen 177, *177*, 180, 181, *181*, 182, 184
Cramtton, Jeff *10*, *186*
Crimson *See* Harvard University.
Crisler, Herbert O 'Fritz' *159*, 159, 160, 161, 175
Crissy, Chris 164, *165*
Crocicchia, Jim 145
Crosby, Joe 104
Crouthamel, Jake *93*, *95*
Crowley, Charles F 41, *42*
Crowley, Paul 108
Crum, Harry 159
Cuccia, Ron 125
Culver, John 108
Cumnock, A J 100
Curtin, Mike *186*, 188
Czinger, Kevin *181*, 182, 183

Daly, Charles 100
Danzig, Allison 67
Dart, Steve 120
Dartmouth College *4*, 6, *8*, *10*, 11, 17, 21, 22, *30*, *32*, 42, *63*, 64, *65*, 66, 67, 67, 68, 69, 70, 71, 72, 80-97, *102*, 102, 108, *111*, 111, 113, 114, 115, *118*, 118, 119, 120, *120*, 125, 129, 136, 139, 142, 144, 145, *145*, *147*, 148, *148*, 153, *153*,

157, 161, *161*, 162, *162*, 163, *163*, 164, 165, 174, 175, 177, 178, 180, 189
Davenport, Tim 123
Davidson, Jack 161
Davis, Gene *138*, 139
Day, Tony 52
DeLamielleure, Jeff *75*, 76
Deland, Lorin 100
Denver, University of 91
Desir, Dexter 145
DeWitt, John 156
DeWitt, Wallace 82
Diana, Rich 183, *183*, 184, 188
Dibblee, Ben 100, *101*
Dickson, Rev Jonathan 152
DiGiacomo, Carm 68
Diller, Jack 173
Dobie, Gilmour 'Gloomy Gil' 62, 64, *64*, 65, 66, 83
Doherty, Pete 178
Domres, Marty 52, *54*
Donelli, Buff 50, 52, *55*
Donovan, Pete 114
Donovan, 'Wild Bill' 43
Dorrance, Jack 69
Dorset, Pete 69
Dowling, Brian 114, 115, 116, 178, *179*
Doyle, Tom 180
Drahos, Nick 67, *67*, 68, 69
Drvanic, Emil 107
Duca, Steve *72*, 76
Dufek, Joe *185*
Duke University 16, 72
Durst, Chuck 125
Durston, Alfred 156

Eckstein, Adolph 'Dolph' *19*, *20*
Ederer, John 108
Eichler, Vince 66
Eliot, Charles W 102
Elis *See* Yale University.
Emery, John 115
Emper, Bill *120*, 121
Engle, Charles 'Rip' 16, *25*, 27
Eton Players 12

Fangmeyer, Jim 145
Farber, Lou 21, *22*
Farley, John 102
Farnham, Bob 32
Farnham, Mike 31, *31*, 32
Farnum, Mark 18, *20*
Fazio, Foge 110
Federspiel, Bob 50
Fencik, Gary 121, 181
Finney, Frank 27, *27*
Fisher, Bob 104, *105*
Fitzgerald, F Scott 157
Fleischmann, Jeff 70
Flippen, Royce 162
Flynn, Chris 145, *146*, 148
Flynn, Wally 107
Folsom, Fred 81, *82*, 82
Fortna, Jeff 145
Frank, Clint 66, 175, *176*
Franklin Field 125, 139, 142, 148, 185
Freeman, Bruce 115, 116
French, Art 104
Frick, Ray *138*, 139
Friesell, Red 89, *91*
Frost, A B *152*

Gammino. Frank 22, *22*
Gannon, Chip 107
Gardner, Harry 157
Garrett, Jason 165, *166*
Garrett, Jim 165
Garrett, John 165
Garrett, Judd 165, *166*

Garrity, Hank 158
Gates, Artemus 173
Gatto, Vic 110, *113*, 113, *115*, 115, 116
Gehrig, Lou *43*
Gelbert, Charles S 132, *133*
George, William 155
Gettysburg College 110
Gilbane, Bill 22
Gilmore, Tom 145
Gizzi, Greg *123*, 128
Glatz, Bob *123*, 129
Glaze, Ralph 81, *82*
Gogolak, Charlie 162, *163*
Gogolak, Pete 68, 71, 92, 163
Goodwin, Bob *166*
Gorman, Johnny 159
Graham, Derek 164, *166*
Grana, Bill 111
Grange, Harold 'Red' *136*, 139
Grant, Wally 177
Gray, Howard 159
Grayson, Bobby 47, 48
Green, Theodore Francis 16
Greenough, Mal *105*
Green. *See* Dartmouth College.
Grieve, Curt *181*, 183, 184
Guarnaccia, Dave 104
Gummere, William S 152

Hadden, Gavin 21
Haggerty, Tom 50
Halaby, Sam 110
Halas, George 48, *48*
Hall, Bob 27
Hall, Irving 'Shine' 22, 25, *25*
Hall, Pete 115
Hallas, Herb 176
Hamilton Park 170
Handrahan, John 87
Hanson, Leonard 'Swede' 62
Harding, Victor 104
Hardwick, Tack *102*
Hare, T Truxton *134*, 134
Harlow, Dick 105, *105*, 106, 107, 110
Harmon, Derrick *13*, *70*, 76
Harmon, Tom 139
Harp, Tom 68, 71, 72
Harper, Jesse 103
Hart, Edward 157
Harvard Stadium 7, 32, 100, *101*, 102, 103, 108, 113, 114, 116, 118, 128, 173, 174, 175, 178, 181, 183
Harvard University 6, *7*, *8*, 10, *10*, 11, 16, 18, 19, 22, 27, 30, 32, 36, 40, 52, *59*, 62, 62, 67, 71, 72, 76, 81, *82*, 82, 84, 87, 89, 91, 92, 94, *95*, 96, 97, 98-129, 134, *135*, 135, 136, 142, 144, *145*, 145, 148, 152, 154, *155*, 156, *157*, 158, 161, *162*, 164, 165, 166, 170, 171, 172, *173*, 173, 174, *175*, 175, 176, *177*, 177, 178, *179*, 181, 182, 185, *186*, 188, 189
Harvard University Committee on the Regulation of Athletic Sports 100
Haughton, Percy 8, 41, *45*, 60, 100, *102*, 103, 104, 172, *173*
Haverford College *45*
Hawken, Sam 92
Hawkes, Dean Herbert 50
Hawley, Jesse 83, 84, 85, 87
Healy, Edward Francis 83, *83*

Heffelfinger, William 'Pudge' *134*, 134, 136, 154, 171, *172*

Heisman, John William 16, 17, 136

Heisman Trophy 16, 72, 136, *161*, 162, 175, *176*

Hickman, Herman 176

Hill, Calvin 116, 178, *178*, *179*

Hillebrand, A R T 'Doc' 156

Hinkey, Frank 171, *173*, 173

Hinz, Tony *125*, 129

Hippenstiel, Brad *132*, 145, *146*, 148

Hobbs, Henry 172

Hodge, Paul 21

Holland, Jerome 'Brud' *65*, 66

Hollenback, Bill 136

Holly, Bob 185

Holmes Field 102

Holt, Mike *118*, 119-20,121

Holy Cross, College of the 32, 88, 91, 115, *118*, 125, 129, 178, 185, *185*

Homans, Steve *173*

Hopkins, Ernest M 85, 89

Hornblower, Ray 113, 115, 116

Horween, Arnold 104, *105*

Howe, Colby *89*

Hughes, Thomas 59

Huguley, Art 105

Hulman, Tony 173

Humenuk, Bill 111

Hunt, Sanford 60

Hurricane Flora game 89, *90*, 161, *161*

Hutchinson, 'Bombshell Bill' 88-9, *89*

Iacavazzi, Cosmo *160*, 163

Illinois, University of 93, 139

Ingerslev, Chris 37, *37*

Ingham, John 81

Intercollegiate Football Association 10, 11

Isom, Bobby *163*, 164

Jackson, Keith 121

Jackson, Levi 176, 177

James, George 'Lefty' 69, *69*, 70, 71

Jardine, Leonard C 27, 29

Jarvis Field 102

Jauron, Dick *169*, 180

Jiggets, Danny 121

Johnson, Charlie 55

Johnson, Jeff *58*, 76, *76*

Jones, Howard 173

Jones, T A D *173*, 173, 174

Jones, Tommy Lee 115

Jones, Tony 185

Jordan, Lloyd 108, *108*, 110

Jordan, Steve 32, *32*

Josephson, Harry 27

Joslin, Jim 108

Kavanagh, Doc 66

Kaw, Eddie 62, *62*, 63, 64

Kazmaier, Dick 'Kaz' 108, 161, *161*, 162

Keenan, Bob *186*

Kelley, Alva 27

Kelley, Larry 175, *176*

Kelley, Robert F 45

Kelly, Bill 116

Kemp, Jeff 97

Kennedy, Edward 'Ted' 108, 113

Kennedy, John F 106, *106*, 113

Kennedy, Robert 113

Kenny, Jack 87

Keohane, Hank 110-11

Kerr, Andy 22

Kevorkian, Alex 105

Kevorkian, Ed 21, *22*

Keys, Brian *147*

Killian, John 76

Kilpatrick, Reed 172

King, F *47*

King, Philip *155*, 155

King, William Haven 91, *92*

Kleinsasser, Bill 161

Klupchak, Rick 94, *95*

Knight, Mike 32

Kohut, Pete 27

Kos, Alex *34*, 37

Koval, George *140*, 142

Krieger, Bob 89

Kubacki, Jim *118*, 120, 121

Kusserow, Lou 50, *50*

Lafayette College 27, 69, 76, 132, 139, 142, 145, 148, 161

Lalich, George 115, 116

Lamar, Henry 106

Lamar, Lilly 154

Lambert Trophy 67, 81, *88*, 89, 91, *92*, 93, 93, *161*, 163, 176

Landers, Hank 32, 36

Landis, Houston 173

Lane, Myles Joseph 85, *86*

Lansberg, Mort 66

Larson, Pete 72

Lassiter, Bob 175

Lawrence, Eddie 21, *22*

Lea, Langdon 'Biffy' 155, *156*

Legore, Harry 173

Lehigh University 13, 59, 71, 134, 156, 166

Lentz, Jim 110

Leo, Bobby 113

Leone, Lew 164

Lewis, Don 55

Lincoln Field 16

Lind, Doug 94

Lindsey, John Hathaway 16, *17*

Lions *See* Columbia University.

Lista, Mike *132*, 145, *145*, 148

Littauer, Lucius 100

Little, Lou 42-3, 45, *45*, 47, *47*, 48, 49, 50

Lockenmeyer, Mark 164

Logan, Mel *102*

Lovejoy, Winslow 174, *174*

Lowenstein, Carroll 108, *108*

Luckman, Sid 25, 47, 48, *48*

Luman, R D *174*

Lynah, Jim 68

Lynch, Ed 83

Lynch, Mike 123

McCall, Bill 87

McCarthy, John *68*

McClung, 'Bum' 171

McConnell, Bruce 145

McConnell, Mike *125*

McCormick, James *156*, 156

McCornack, Walter *80*, 81

McCullough, Hal 67, *67*

McDermott, Bob 123

McElhenny, Hugh 162

McFadden, Jerry *145*

McGill, Dennis 176, *177*

McGill University 12, 84, 100

McGinley, Ed 136

McHale, Tom 70, 75, 76

McLaughry, DeOrmond 'Tuss' 21, *22*, 22, *88*, 89

McLaughry, John 25, *25*, 27, 29

McLean, John 163

MacLeod, Robert 'Wildfire' 87, 88, 89, *89*

MacLeod, Russell 69

Macauley, Ted 186

Macdonald, Torbert 106

Madden, Pat 178

Mahan, Eddie *102*, 103

Mallory, William 173, 174

Manley, Phil *182*

Marchant, Reginald 69

Margarita, Bob 16, *25*, 27

Marinaro, Ed 70, 72, *72*, 76, 93

Marion, Roland 68

Maroon, S *47*

Maroons *See* University of Chicago.

Marsters, Al 'Special Delivery' *86*

Martinez-Zorilla, José C 65, *65*

Marting, Walt 114

Mason, Frank 100

Masterson, Tom *165*

Matal, Tony 46

Matuszak, Walt 67

Maxwell Award 142, *161*

Mayhew, John 17, *20*

Mercein, Chuck 177

Metcalf, T Nelson 41, *41*

Metropoulos, Ted 108

Metzger, Sol 136

Michalko, Paul 31, *31*, 32

Michie Stadium 48

Michigan, University of 11, 18, 69, 70, 136, *139*, 139, 154, 156, 160, 171, 175, 184

Middlebury College 29

Miller, Howard 41, *42*

Miller, Neal 121

Milstead, Century 174

Minds, John Henry 'Jack' *133*, 134

Minisi, Skippy 139

Minnesota, University of 156, 159

Minnesota Vikings 32, *32*, 72

Mishel, Dave 21, *22*, 22

Mitchell, Ledyard 156

Moffat, Alex 154, *155*

Molloy, Ed 176

Montgomery, Cliff 43, 45, 46, *46*, 47

Moravec, Vince 106

Moriarty, Kevin 186, *188*

Morley, Bill *40*, 40

Morris, Seth 29, 30, *31*

Morris, Tom 162

Morton, Craig 96

Morton, William 'Air Mail' *86*, 87

Mosely, George 173

Moyle, Wallace *80*, 81

Munger, George *138*, 139, 142

Murphy, Gerry 27, 29, 68

Murrey, Frank 158

Musick, Jack 68, 70, 72, 76

Nairne, Pop 87

Nash, Tom 25

National Football Conference 32

National Football Hall of Fame 16, *18*, 18, 59, 60, 62, 65, 66, 69, 76, 81, 83, 85, 87, 89, 102, 136, *140*

National Football League 12, 32, 116, 142, *178*, 178

Navarro, Frank 52, *55*

Navy (U.S. Naval Academy) 67, 106, *139*, 139, 142, 145, *145*, 148, 157, 161, 175, *180*, *181*, 183, *183*, 184, *185*

Neidlinger, Pudge 83

Nelson, Scott 31

Nelson, Spike 175

Nelson, Swede 106

Nitti, John 183, *183*

Nevel, B *47*

Newell, Marshall 59, 60, 100

New Jersey, College of 153, 154

New York Giants 25

New York Jets 32

New York University *45*, 161

Nolan, Chuck 145

Northeastern University 128

Northwestern University 40, 87

Notre Dame, University of 103, *139*, 142, 173

Novoselsky, Brent 148

Oberlander, Andrew 'Swede' 83, 84, 85

O'Connor, J C 82

O'Connor, Tom 50, *52*

Odell, Howie 175, *176*, 176

O'Donnell, Cleo 106

O'Hearn, Charlie 173

O'Hearn, John 60, *60*

Ohio State University 66, 68, 139

O'Keefe, Ken 30

Olivar, Jordan 176, *177*, 177

O'Neil, Gil 108

O'Neill, Brendan 93

O'Neill, Mike 145

Oregon, University of 136, *136*

Owens, Jesse 89

Pagliaro, John *180*, 181, 182

Palmer Stadium 7, 89, 161, *161*, 163, 164

Parilli, Babe 162

Parkhurst, Lewis 81

Parry, John 27

Pasadena City College 91

Paterno, Joe 16, *25*, 27

Peabody, Endicott 'Chub' 106, *107*

Pennock, Stan *102*

Pennsylvania State University 16, 36, 136, 139, 142, 163

Pennsylvania, University of 4, 6, 8, 10, *13*, 16, *17*, 30, 32, 42, 49, 52, *58*, 59, 60, 62, 64, 66, 67, 68, 69, 70, 71, 75, 76, 76, 89, 91, 93, 94, 97, *101*, 115, 125, 128, 132-48, *152*, 154, 155, 161, 164, 166, 174, 176, 177, 180, 181, 185, 188, 189

Percy Field 59

Perry, Ted 94, *95*

Pfann, George 62, *62*, 64, *65*

Philbin, Steve 172

Pierce, Chester *106*, 107

Pittsburgh University 22, 139, 183

Poderys, Eric *147*

Poe, Arthur 155, 156

Poe, Edgar Allan 154

Poe, Gresham 155

Poe, John P Jr 'Johnny' 155, 156, *156*

Poe, Nielson 155

Poe, S Johnson 155

Pollard, Frederick 'Fritz' 19, *20*, 173

Pollock, Bill 94

Pond, Raymond 'Ducky' 175

Pont, John 177, *177*

Porter, Cole 170

Potkul, Jamie *34*, 36, 37

Potter, Joe *16*, 36

Prassas, John 32

Prentice Cup 104

Princeton University 4, 6, 7, 8, 10, 11, 30, 31, *31*, 32, 40, 43, 52, 55, 60, 67, *67*, 70, 71, 72, *72*, 76, 82, 87, 88, 89, *90*, 91, 92, 93, 94, 100, *100*, 106, *107*, 107, 108, *108*, 111, *111*, 113, 115, 118, 119, *123*, 125, *129*, 129, 139, 142, *143*, 144, 148, 152-66, 170, 171, 172, *173*, 173, 174, 175, 177, 178, 180, 182, 185, 186, 188, *188*, 189

Pugh, Wesley 94

Purdy, Clair 18, *20*

Pyle, Mike 176

Quakers *See* Pennsylvania, University of.

Radvilas (Columbia-Army 1938) 48

Rams *See* Rhode Island, University of.

Ramsay, Floyd 62, *62*

Randall, Joe 27, *27*

Randall, Roy 'Red' 21, *22*

Ravreby, Fred 108

Ray, Carl 'Mutt' 87

Raymond, Walter 18

Reagan, Frank *138*, *139*, 139

Reed, Fritz 116

Regio, Bill 55

Reid, Bill 100, 102, 103

Reja, Ron 76

Restic, Joe *117*, 118, 119, 120, *120*, 125, 128, 129

Rhode Island, University of 30, *31*, 31, 37

Richeson, Lyle 174

Riggs, Jesse 155

Rissman, J *47*

Ritter, Chris 72

Roberts, Archie Jr *52*, 52

Robertson, Jim 83

Robinson, Edward North 'Robbie' 16, *18*, 19, 21

Robinson, Roger 110

Rochester Institute of Technology 59

Rockefeller, John D Jr 16, *19*

Rockne, Knute 67, 85, *105*

Rogan, John *180*, 181, 182, 183, 184

Rogerson, Ron 165, *166*

Rohrer, Jeff 184

Rooney, Kevin 32

Roosevelt, Theodore 102-03

Root, Reggie 175

Roper, William W *157*, 158, 159

Rorke, Chris 96

Rose Bowl 16, 18, 22, 40, 43, 45, *47*, 47, 64, 67, 69, 70, 89, 104, 108, 136, *136*, *160*

Rosenberg, John *34*, 36, 37

Rossides, Gene 50, *50*

Rostomily, Bob 182

Rutgers University 8, 10, 11, 40, 64, 120, 142, *152*, 153, 163, *164*

Ryan, Kelly 186, *188*, 188

Ryzewics, Gene 113

Sage, Heinie 85

St John, Burke 123

St Lawrence University 41

St Pierre, Dave 118

Santini, Gerry 142

Savitsky, George 139
Saxton, Harold 18, *20*
Scarlett, Hunter 136
Schoellkopf Field 60, 64, 70,76
Schoellkopf, Henry 'Heinie' 60, *60*
Scholl, Walter 'Pop' 67, *67*, 68
Schulz, 'Germany' 136
Sciolla, Joe 120
Sebastianelli, A J 145
Sebo, Steve *140, 142*, 142
Seidenberg, Hal 70
Seifert, George 72, 76
Sharpe, Al 60, 62, *62*, 173
Shaughnessy, Robert 'Shag' 110, *111*
Shaverick, Fritz 62
Sheerer, Hank 158
Shelton, Murray 62
Shevlin, Tom 171, 173
Short, John 93
Shula, David 97, *97*, 125
Simourian, John 108
Singleterry, Gary 115
Singleton, Tom 176, 177
Slattery, Kevin 30
Smith, Andy 136
Smith, Ken 158
Smith, Orland 21, *22, 40*
Smock, L P 153
Snavely, Carl *64*, 65, 66, 67, 68, 69, 69
Soldiers Field 102, 110
Solomon, Jimmy *120*
Spangenberg, Tom 91
Spears, Clarence 83
Spike, Edgar J 18, *20*
Sprackling, Bill 16, 17, *20*
Sprague, Ken 18, *20*
Stagg, Amos Alonzo 59, *59*, 85, *157, 159, 171, 172*

Stanczyk, Leslie *48*
Stanford, George Foster 40
Stanford University 18, 45, 46, 47, *47*, 48, 87, 89, *100*
Starbuck, Raymond 60
Stark, Pat 110
Stephens, Chalmers 81
Stephens, Tom 110
Stetson, Steve 94
Stevens, Mal 174, 175
Stevenson, Vincent 134, 135, *135*
Stewart, Dan 29
Stewart, George 100
Stiegman, John *142*, 142
Stitt, Herbert D *156*
Stoeckel, Jim *117*, 118, 119
Struck, Vernon 106
Sullivan, Mike 182
Sullivan, Pat 72
Sundstrom, Frank 'Sunny' *62*, 62, 65
Suren, Dan 76
Swarthmore College 132
Sweitzer, Ken *181*
Swiacki, Bill *50*, 50
Syracuse University 66, 67, 68, 69, 71
Szaro, Richie 116

Team of Destiny *157*, 158, 160, *161*
Teevens, Eugene 'Buddy' *96*, 97
T-formation 48
Thomas, Chuck 94
Thomas, John *158*, 159
Thomas, 'Whitey' 157
Thompson, Oliver 153
Thorpe, Jim *20*
Ticknor, Ben 104
Tigers *See* Princeton University.

Tiley, Fred 162
Tino, Marcello *68*
Torrey, Bob 134-35
Tosches, Steve 165
Tournament of Roses *20 See also* Rose Bowl.
Towle, Thurston 21, *22*
Traub, Bill 27
Trevor, George 134
Trimble, Maury 157, 158
Trumbull, Wally *102*
Tumpane, Tim 182
Tyler, Bob 89

Union College, Schenectady, NY 59
U.S. Military Academy *See* Army.
U.S. Naval Academy *See* Navy.

Valpey, Arthur 107, 108
Van Pelt, Larry 164, *165*
Varney, Pete *115*, 115, 116
Vasell, Tom 50
V-formation 91
Villela, Rick 32
Violante, José 29, 30, 37
Virginia, University of 106-07, *136*, 139

Wade, W Wallace 'Wally' 16, 18, *20*
Walter, Scott 76
Ward, Ray 18, *20*
Warner, Glenn 'Pop' 58, *59*, 59, 60, 102
Warner, William 60, 62
Warren, Russ 50
Washington and Jefferson College 173
Washington State University 18, *20*, 62, 83, 162

Webster, Steve 94
Weekes, Harold 40, 135
Weeks, Josh 18, *20*
Wendell, Percy 103
Wesleyan University 16, 41
West, Fred 66
Western Reserve 64
Wharton, Charles 'Buck' *133*, 134
Wheeler, Arthur 155, 156
Whidden, Tim 29
Whipple, Mark *31*, 32
White, Andrew D 59
White, Ed 79
White, Sam 157
Whiting, Allen E 59
Whitney, Caspar 154
Wieman, E E 'Tad' 160
Wilbur, Jack 105
William and Mary, College of 36, 152, 188
Williams, Carl *133*, 134, 135
Williams College 64
Williams, Reginald 94
Williams, William 'Big Bill' 156
Wilson, Donald 145, 148
Winchester, Dana 'Win' 132
Wing-T offense 27
Winn, Tommy 120, *120*, 121
Winterbaur, Dick 176
Withington, Paul 41
Witkowski, John 55, *55*
Wittmer, Al 159
Wolfe, Kenny 177
Wolverines *See* University of Michigan.
Wood, Gary *68*, 71
Wood, W Barry *104*, 104-05, 175
Woodring, John 32, 36
Woodruff, George 134, *134*
Wright, Jim 40

Wyckoff, Clinton *60*, 60
Wylie, Red 108

Yablonski, Ventan 50
Yale Bowl *12*, 114, 119, 123, *157*, 170, 174, 175, 182, *185*, 185, 186
Yale, Elihu 170
Yale University 4, 6, *7, 8, 10*, 10, 11, 17, 18, 19, *20*, 21, 27, 29, 30, 31, 32, *34*, 36, 37, *40*, 40, *48*, 52, *54*, 59, 64, 65, 66, 68, 69, 71, 72, 75, 87, *88*, 89, 92, 93, 97, 100, *101*, 102, 103, *104*, 105, 106, 108, 110, 111, 113, 114, *115*, 115, 116, 118, 120, 121, 123, *123*, 125, 128, *128*, 129, 132, 134, *135*, 135, 136, 139, 142, 144, 148, *152*, 152, 153, *154*, 154, 155, 156, *157*, 157-58, 159, *159*, 160, 161, 162, 163, 166, *168*, *169*, 170-88, 189
Yeager, Charles 108, 176, *177*
Yohe, Tom *100, 123*, 128, 129
Yost, Fielding 'Hurry-Up' 136
Yovicsin, John 110, 111, 113, 114, *115*, 116, *117*, 117, 118
Yukica, Joe 94, 96, 97

Zbrzeznj, Bernie 142
Zimmerman, Ric *113*, 113, 114, 115
Zitrides, Gregory 'Gus' 87
Zubrow, Ed 145

ACKNOWLEDGMENTS
The publisher wishes to thank the following people who have helped in the preparation of this book: Jeffrey H. Orleans and Connie Huston of the Council of Ivy Group Presidents; librarians, archivists, and sports information offices of several of the colleges and universities; Jean Chiaramonte Martin, editor; Janet Wu York, assistant editor; Mike Rose, designer; Donna Cornell Muntz, picture editor; and Florence Norton, who prepared the index.

PICTURE CREDITS
The Bettmann Archive, Inc: pages 1, 8(both), 9(top left), 12(left), 40(bottom), 44(top), 45(bottom), 90(top), 100(right), 101(center), 103(top), 105(bottom left), 107(top), 152(top left & bottom), 155(bottom left), 168, 174(all three), 175(both), 176(top right).
Brown University Archives: pages 16, 17(all three), 18(both), 19(both), 20(top right & bottom), 21(both), 22, 23(bottom right), 25(bottom left), 26(bottom two), 36(top).
Brown University Sports Information Office: pages 22-23, 23(bottom left), 24, 25(top, bottom center & right), 26(top), 27, 29(both), 30, 31(top left & bottom), 32(top left), 33, 36(bottom); Dick Benjamin 28; Thomas F Maguire Jr 6(left), 10(bottom right), 14-15, 20(top left), 32(top right), 34(all four), 35, 37(both); Danya Powers 31(top right).
Columbia University Sports Information: pages 38-39, 53(both).
Cornell University Sports Information Office: pages 10(top), 58(both), 59, 60(all three), 61, 62-63(all four), 64(both), 65(all three), 68(bottom), 69(both), 70(both), 71(top), 72(left); Jonathan J Barkey 77; Jon Crispin 12-13; Russ Hamilton 72(right); Fred Keib 68(top); Tim McKinney 11(top), 75(bottom right), 76.
CW Pack Sports: pages 56-57, 71(bottom), 73, 74, 75(top & bottom left).
Dartmouth College Library: pages 4-5, 9(top right), 80(top & bottom left), 81, 82(all three), 83(bottom), 84-85, 86(top & bottom right), 87, 88-89, 90(bottom), 92(bottom), 95(top), 96(bottom left).
Dartmouth College Sports Information: pages 6(right), 10(bottom left), 80(bottom right), 83(top two), 88(both), 92(top), 93(both), 94(top), 94-95; H/O Photographers Inc

78-79(both), 96(top & right center); Kathy Slattery 97.
Harvard University Sports News Bureau: pages 98-99, 100(left), 101(top), 102, 103(bottom), 104, 105(top), 106(bottom), 107(bottom), 110, 111(both), 113(both), 117(bottom right), 118(both); Dick Raphael 112, 114(bottom), 115, 116-17, 119(top), 125(left); Savage Photo 108; Chris Stafford 119(bottom).
Paul Huegel: pages 166(center right & bottom), 167(bottom).
John F Kennedy Library: page 106(top).
Ed Mahan Photo: pages 147(both), 148-49(both).
Karen Morse: page 127
Tim Morse: pages 7(top left), 11(bottom), 98, 121, 122, 123(all three), 124, 125(right), 126(all three), 128, 129(both), 187.
The National Football Foundation and Hall of Fame: page 40(top).
The New York Public Library Picture Collection: pages 101(bottom), 154, 171(top).
University of Pennsylvania Sports Information: pages 13(right), 130-31, 132, 133(all three), 134, 135(both), 136, 137(both), 138(both), 139, 140(both), 141, 142, 143(both), 144-45(all three), 146(both), 189(right).
Princeton University Office of Athletic Communications: pages 2-3, 7(top right, center left & bottom), 9(top right, center left & bottom), 150-51, 152(top right), 153, 155(top & bottom right), 156(all four), 157(left), 158(top), 159(top), 160-61(all five), 162(top & center), 163(both), 164, 165(right), 166(top & center left), 167(top).
Pro-Football Hall of Fame: page 172(bottom).
UPI/Bettmann Newsphotos: pages 9(bottom), 41, 42(both), 43(both), 44(bottom), 45(top), 46(all three), 47(both), 48(both), 49(both), 50, 51(both), 52, 54(both), 55(both), 66(both), 67(both), 86(bottom left), 91, 96(bottom right), 105(bottom right), 109(both), 114(top), 117(top right), 120-21(both), 157(right two), 158(bottom), 159(bottom), 162(bottom), 165(left).
Yale Sports Publicity: pages 7(center right), 169, 170(both), 171(bottom), 172(top two), 173(all three), 176(top left, top center & bottom), 177(all four), 178(both), 179, 180(all three), 181(both), 182, 183(both), 184(both), 185, 186(both), 188(both), 189(left).